The Pattern Library

RUGS AND WALL HANGINGS

The Pattern Library

RUGS AND WALL HANGINGS

Editor
Debra Maltzman Grayson

BALLANTINE BOOKS · NEW YORK

First published in Great Britain in 1984 by
Ebury Press, National Magazine House,
72 Broadwick Street, London W1V 2BP

The Pattern Library RUGS AND WALL HANGINGS was conceived,
edited and designed by Dorling Kindersley Limited,
9 Henrietta Street, London WC2

Published in the United States by Ballantine Books,
a division of Random House, Inc., New York,
and simultaneously in Canada by Random House
of Canada, Limited, Toronto, Canada.

Library of Congress Catalog Card Number: 84–90817

ISBN 0–345–31867–6

Manufactured in the United States of America

First Ballantine Books Edition: October 1984
10 9 8 7 6 5 4 3 2 1

Contents

Introduction

The increased use of handicrafts as both practical and decorative items in the home has encouraged a great revival of hand-made rugs and wall hangings. Probably the most appealing aspects of this craft are the limitless opportunities for creativity, experimentation and originality. There are no set rules regarding the use of color, pattern or texture.

Most of the rugs shown can also be displayed as wall hangings, and vice-versa – it's up to you to decide. While instructions are provided, the works shown on the following pages may simply give you ideas for rugs and wall hangings you can create by using the same basic techniques.

The origins of rug-making date back to at least 2000 B.C. Rugs were nearly all made by tying short lengths of yarn on to the warp threads of a loom to create a piled fabric. The Scandinavians worked shaggy piled rugs in unwashed woolen yarns, and, because they stood up to water so much better than animal skins, they were used by fishermen as raincoats. Their thickness and warmth meant that they were also used as wall hangings to keep out the drafts and as floor coverings and bedspreads.

Hooked rugs also originated in Scandinavia. The Vikings used fur-like piled fabrics as clothing to withstand the cold. They took the technique to the British Isles, and hand-hooking became a very popular craft in the North East of England, where the local mills and cloth factories made materials easily available. "Hooky mats", made with long strips of cloth often cut from old clothes or blankets, were hooked into burlap with the loops showing on the finished side. "Proddy mats", also called "proggy" or "clippy" mats, were worked by pushing (or prodding) the ends of short strips of cloth through the burlap from the wrong side, so that the ends stood out on the right side. A northern family's best mats were reserved for weekends and special occasions. During the week, old mats were used, especially in doorways for picking up dirt from the farmer's boots.

British settlers introduced the craft in the American colonies, where it flourished. Some of the most beautiful hooked rugs date from eighteenth- and early nineteenth-century New England. They, too, were hooked with thin strips of used fabric. The bold, colorful designs portrayed flowers, animals and landscapes, and have become notable representatives of American folk art.

The simple techniques included in this book can be learned quickly and easily, with a minimal amount of tools and materials. The designs can be closely imitated, or adapted to your own tastes – the possibilities are endless.

BASIC TECHNIQUES

EQUIPMENT

Little equipment is required to make beautiful hooked, braided and woven rugs. The tools and materials needed are listed under each separate technique on the following pages.

Part of the joy of rug-making is in the ready availability of materials – not only are art-supply shops well stocked with a variety of yarns, hooks and frames, but very often rug materials can be found in the home, as leftover sewing scraps and old clothes are ideal for hooked rag rugs.

DESIGNING YOUR OWN RUG

Rug design can take the form of anything from abstract shapes to formal borders to pictorial scenes of animals and landscapes. There are two methods of working out a design. You can either draw the shapes onto the backing fabric on the side that you are working with an indelible crayon or you can lay out the design on graph paper. The first method is better for hand hook and punch hook techniques on fabric backings; the second is more suited to open-mesh canvas rugs such as latch hook and needlepoint. (For woven rugs, we recommend placing a drawing behind the warp threads as a guide.)

Drawing out the design on the backing

Begin by drawing the pattern on to the backing fabric in pencil. Trace around cut-out cardboard shapes if you like. Go over the outlines with an indelible crayon or felt-tipped pen. Remember that any small details in your design will be obscured if you are working a long-piled rug.

Drawing out the design on graph paper
Draw out the design on graph paper. Then go over it and square it off as shown. Each square on the paper represents one stitch, loop or knot. Establish a color code to identify the colors of yarn.

TRANSFERRING DESIGNS

A pattern can easily be transferred to open-mesh canvas. Transfer the outline, and either use your original colored pattern as a color guide, or fill in the colors with waterproof acrylic paint. An easy way to do this is by using a sheet of glass placed between two chairs with a strong lamp underneath.

1 *Tape the colored pattern to the glass. Place the canvas on top of the glass, lining up the vertical or horizontal lines of canvas with those on your design.*

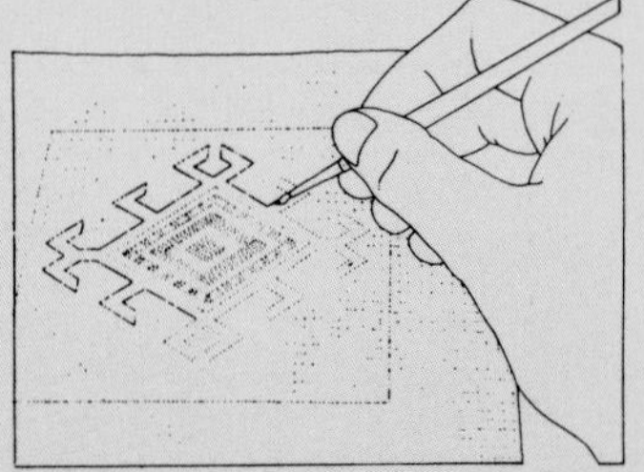

2 *Outline the design using a thin brush and waterproof ink.*

BACKINGS

The *backing* is the foundation on which the rug is worked. The stronger your backing fabric, the better. All hand-made rugs involve a lot of work and this would be wasted if the backing canvas wore out before the surface. When buying, you should choose the one most suitable for your technique. Before starting any rug, work a small sample so that any practical problems can be sorted out early.

BINDING

If the backing finishes with a raw edge, it must be bound and hemmed to prevent it from fraying or unravelling. Sew on a strip of rug binding or tape. Begin by sewing the rug binding on the right side of the backing close to the edge of the rug stitches. Use strong thread and running or back stitch. Cut off the excess backing to within about 1in. on each side. Fold the edges to the back and sew the binding to the back of the rug, making sure that the stitches do not show on the surface. Miter the corners. When binding round or oval rugs, use bias strips. Turn the hems to the back and ease them around the curves by making small, V-shapedd slits in the backing.

LINING

Rugs worked on stiff canvas should not need lining. However, if you do want to line your rug, use heavy burlap or any strong, closely woven fabric. Cut out a piece of fabric 2in. larger all around than the rug. Turn back the edges of unworked canvas to make a hem. Pin the lining at intervals to the back of the rug, starting at the center and working outwards. Check that the grain of the lining and the canvas is the same. Sew the lining to the hem of the rug about ¾in. from the edge on each side using strong thread and herringbone stitch.

For unlined hooked rugs, apply a latex backing to make the rug slip-proof and to stabilize the stitches. Spread the latex very thinly on to the back of the rug using a paintbrush. Trim the unworked edges of canvas down to about 2in. on each side. The corners can be either mitered or folded. Stitch down with cotton or linen carpet thread or use a special adhesive to paste the hem securely to the back of the rug.

Hand hooked rugs

The hand hooked method is the simplest of rug-making techniques and was the one used in the working of traditional rag rugs. Apart from its handle, the hand hook is very similar to a crochet hook. It works by pulling the yarn up through the backing fabric to form loops on the surface. Hooked rugs are firm and durable, and can be vacuumed and/or cleaned.

Hand hook

EQUIPMENT

Backings

Any even, firmly woven fabric with apparent warp and weft threads is suitable. An even-weave mixture of cotton and linen is the best. Burlap can be a little too weak and uneven to give good results, although it was the traditional backing fabric for American hooked rugs.

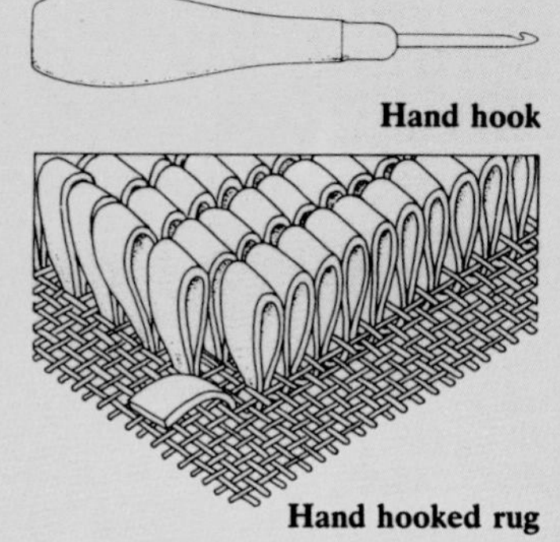

Hand hooked rug

Yarns

Thin strips of cloth make the best yarns, as this hook tends to separate the strands of rug wools when pulling them through the backing.

Frame

The backing fabric should be stretched tautly over a frame to ensure even hooking. Frames are available in various sizes, or you can make your own. Secure the work to them with strong thumb-tacks.

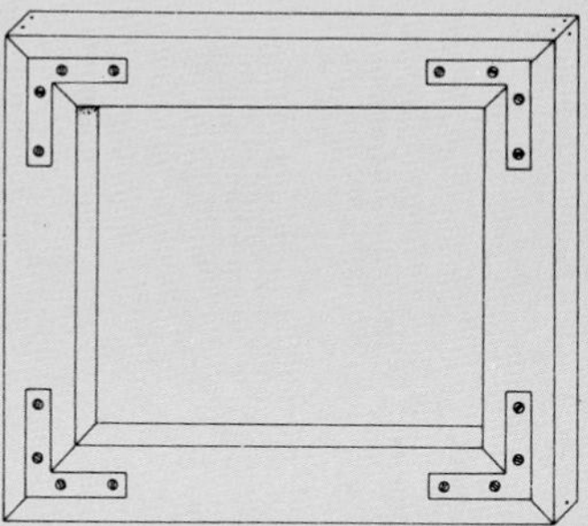

Small lap frame
A simple frame can be made from wooden strips. Miter the corners, nail the pieces into a rectangle and reinforce with metal brackets.

PREPARING THE FABRIC

Wash the fabric first – whether you have bought it new or whether you plan to use old scraps of material. If you are using old clothes, remove any buttons or zippers and open up all the seams and hems. Do not worry if the fabric shrinks: it will be less likely to fray or unravel. Now cut the fabric into strips. The width of the strips will depend on the type of fabric, the kind of backing you are using and the effect you want to achieve. The thinner the strips, the finer the rug. Experiment with different widths: flannels and fairly fine fabrics can be cut to about ½in. wide; medium-weight woven materials to about ¼in. and heavier tweeds and wools can be as thin as ⅛in.

How to cut the strips

Use a pair of sharp scissors. Cut woven fabrics along the grain and knitted fabrics along their length.

If you must join strips together, lay two at right angles, stitch across the top of the diagonal, open up the seam and trim off the edges.

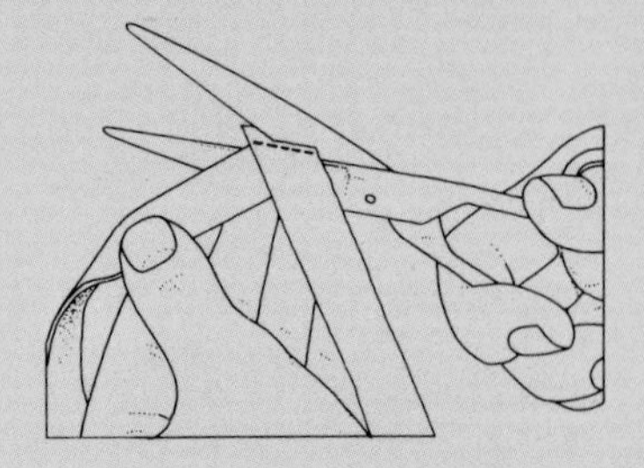

HOOKING

The right side of the backing should be facing up. In this method, the yarn strip of fabric is held beneath the work. The hook is then inserted through the back and the yarn pulled through from the underside to the top in small loops. With practice you can hook in any direction and thus create linear patterns or rhythms in the pile. Always hold the hook in the direction you are working.

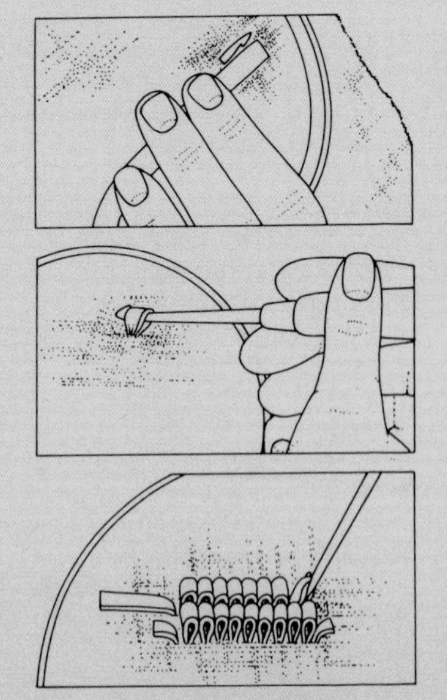

1 *Hold the yarn or the strip of fabric beneath the backing so that it is taut. Push the hook down through the backing from the right side, passing it between warp and weft threads.*

2 *Hook around the yarn and pull it up through the backing to form a loop of the desired height on the right side. It may be difficult at the beginning to make the loops even in height, but by hooking slowly and carefully, you will soon regulate the height without any trouble.*

3 *Advance the hook by one or two backing threads and push it through again ready to pull up another loop. Continue in this way, always starting and finishing a length of yarn by pulling the ends up to the top. The ends can be cut down later to lie lower than the pile of the rest of the rug.*

Prodded rugs

These are thicker and heavier than hooked rugs, and simple or abstract designs are best, since small details will not show through. This type of rug is worked with the wrong side facing you.

EQUIPMENT

The materials are virtually the same as those used in making hand hooked rugs, except for the "prodder" itself, which has a rounded tip.

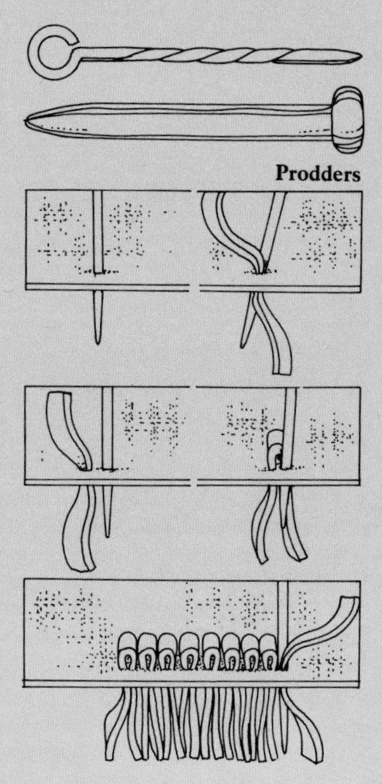

Prodders

PRODDING

1 *Cut rags into strips of approximately 1½in. long by ¾in. wide. Poke a hole in one corner of the burlap with the prodder. Then use the prodder to push one end of a cloth strip through the hole. (Push half of the strip through.)*

2 *Poke a second hole about ½in. away from the first hole and prod the other end of the strip through this hole. Check the right side of the burlap to see that both ends of the strip are equal. Poke one end of another strip into the second hole, which you have already used.*

3 *Poke a third hole about ½in. away from the second hole, and push the remaining end of the strip through it. Continue in this way in straight rows, being careful to place the strips close together. This will ensure that they are in securely and won't come out.*

Latch hooked rugs

These are made by knotting lengths of yarn onto an open-mesh canvas, resulting in a dense piled rug. The height of the pile can be varied either by using different lengths of yarn or by trimming certain areas when complete. Since small details tend to get lost, simple designs are best. No frame is needed.

Latch hook

EQUIPMENT

Backings

The open-mesh canvas of doubled threads is available in gauges of 3–5 holes per inch.

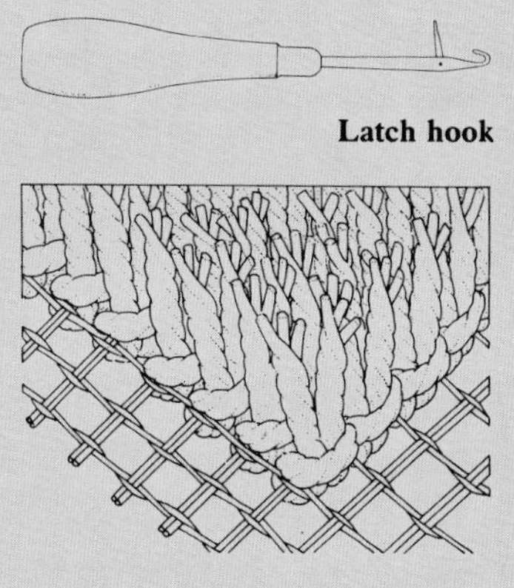

Latch hooked rug

Yarns
Any yarn that fits through the canvas mesh when doubled can be used. The minimum length convenient for hooking is 2½in. which works into a pile of about 1in. Pre-cut yarn can be bought in packets, but it is cheaper to buy skeins of yarn and cut it yourself.

HOOKING

Begin by trying a few sample knots to test out the length and thickness of your yarns. Work horizontally, starting at the bottom and hooking along each row. All the knots should face the same way. Check that every space in the backing canvas has been filled.

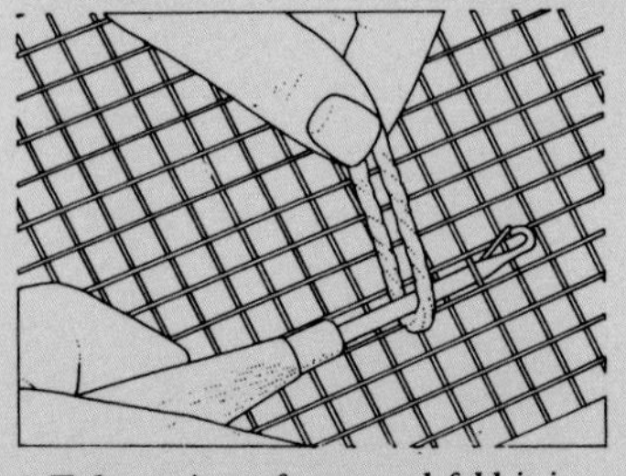

1 *Take a piece of yarn and fold it in half around the shaft of the hook. Now insert the hook and pass it up underneath one horizontal canvas thread.*

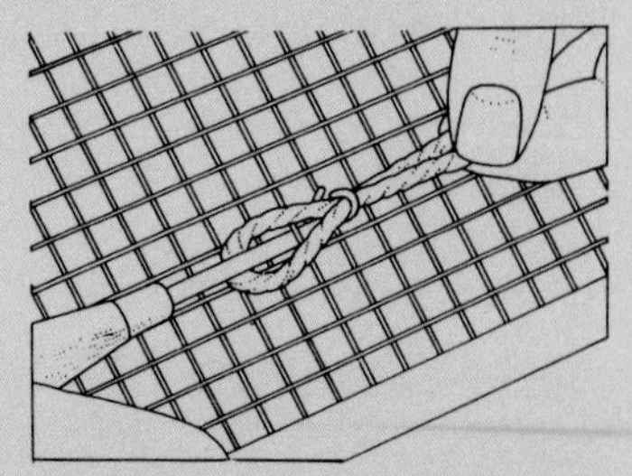

2 *Take the two ends of yarn through the open latch and tuck them down under the hook itself.*

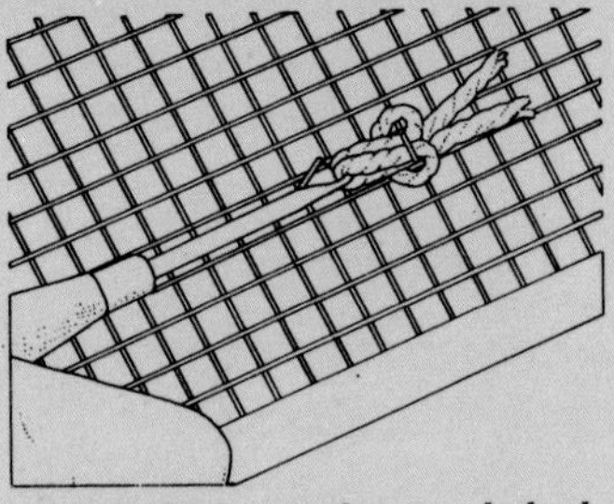

3 *Pull the hook towards you so the latch closes around the yarn. Continue pulling until both ends of the yarn have been drawn through the loop to form the completed knot.*

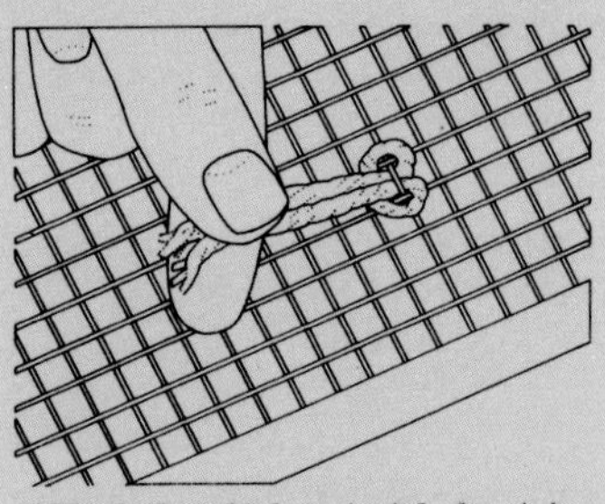

4 *Check that the knot is tight by giving the two ends of the yarn a sharp tug.*

Finishing
A lining is not strictly necessary. However, protect the edges by making a hem of about 1–2in. to the right side. This is done at the beginning of the work. The rug will be more hard-wearing if you also sew a strip of rug binding over the back of the hem on all sides.

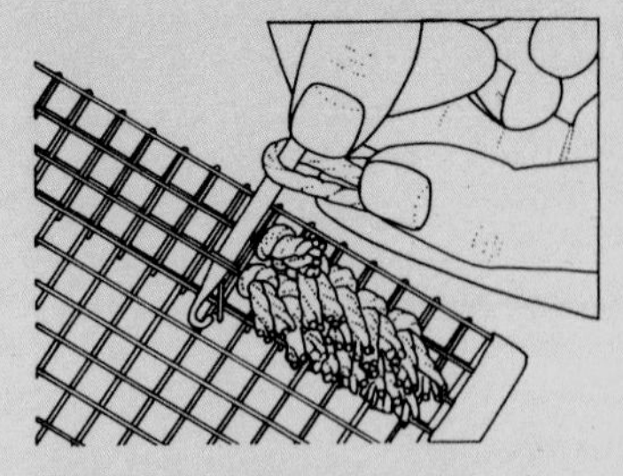

Fold the hem allowance up over the right side of the canvas. Align the warp and weft threads and work through the double thickness.

Punch hooked rugs

This technique is worked with the backing stretched on a frame and with what will be the underside of the rug towards you. The loops are then pushed through from the back to the front and their height is regulated automatically by the punch hook.

EQUIPMENT

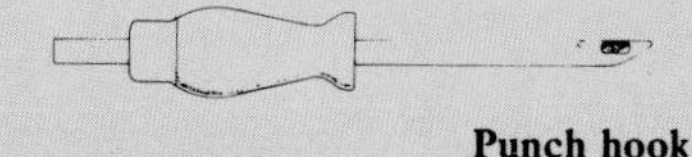

Punch hook

Backings

Any strong, evenly woven fabric is suitable for punch hooking as long as the threads will allow the hook to pass through. Burlap and evenweave cotton/linen are probably the most commonly used backings. If you choose burlap, use the heavy variety.

Yarns

Yarns are easier to use than strips of fabric since they will slide more freely up and down the center of the hook. Various thicknesses and combinations of yarns used together produce interesting textures, and there is scope for using novelty yarns, braids and ribbons as well.

HOOKING

The punch hook is a large hollow needle with an eye on one side of the tube. The size of the loop that it makes can be adjusted from about ¼in. to ¾in. by a turning and locking movement of the wooden handle. The most important thing to remember is not to lift the hook above the surface when you pull it out of the backing.

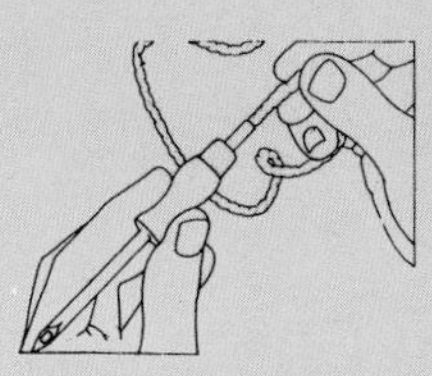

1 *Holding the slotted side of the hook towards you, insert the end of the yarn down into the hollow hook from the top to the bottom.*

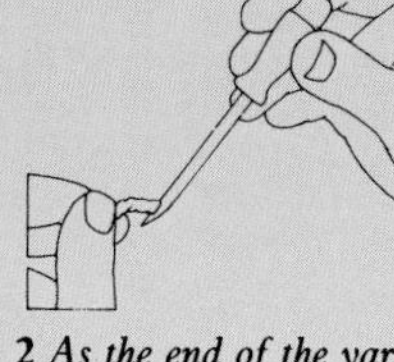

2 *As the end of the yarn appears, thread it through the eye. Make sure that the yarn is free to move through the hook with ease.*

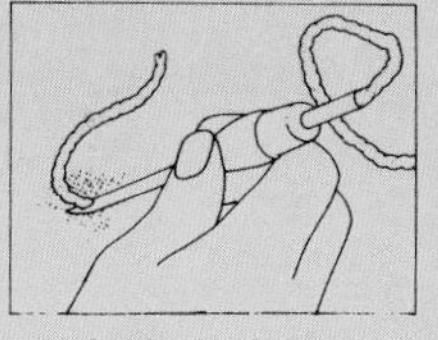

3 *Hold the hook in an upright position, like a pencil. Keep the slotted side facing in the direction you are going.*

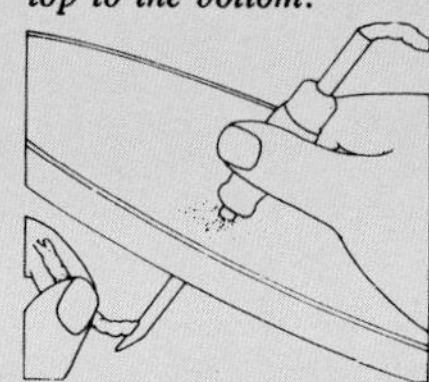

4 *Push the hook down through the backing, between the warp and weft threads, until it will not go any further.*

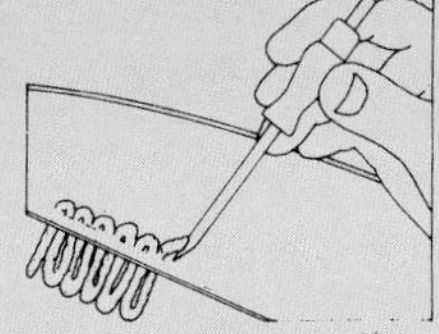

5 *Hold the backing steady and withdraw the hook. Slide it along two or three threads and plunge it in again.*

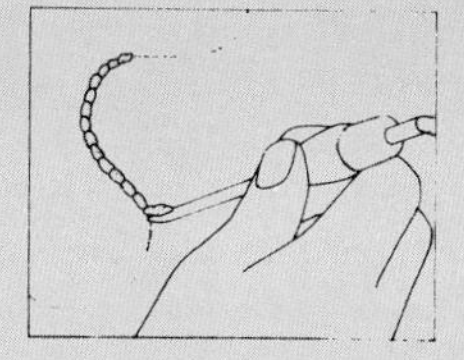

6 *Continue, changing direction when necessary. To change colors, cut yarn short and poke it through to the right side.*

Spacing The spacing between loops will affect the finished look of the work. For a thick, dense look try to keep the spacing even throughout, and don't let the backing show through. Of course, the thickness of the yarn will also dictate the spacing. It might help to try a few practice rows first.

Needlepoint rugs

EQUIPMENT

Backing

Use rug canvas, which has a large, clearly defined mesh of very strong glazed threads. The gauge is measured by the number of holes per inch. Any gauge rug canvas can be used, but one that has 13 holes per inch will give medium-sized stitches.

Threads

Four-ply tapestry wool is most suitable with 13 gauge canvas. However, three strands of crewel wool threaded through the needle at once is also suitable.

Needles

These are available in a range of sizes, but generally, size 20 is a good one to use with 4-ply tapestry wool.

Frame

It is not essential to work on a frame, although this does help to keep your canvas in better shape while you work, and the finished piece should not need as much stretching as one that has not been worked on a frame.

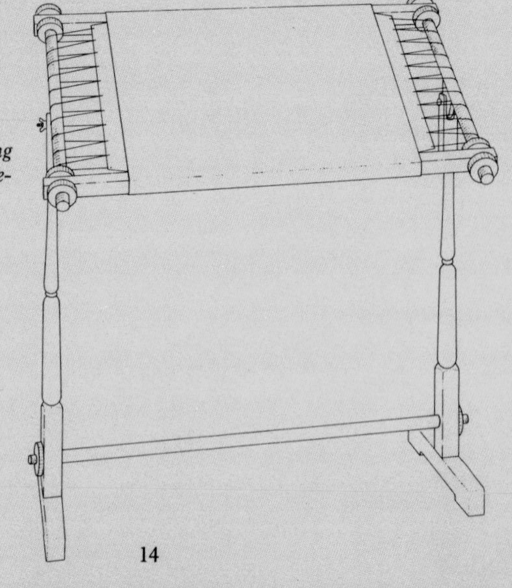

Adjustable frame
This frame is the best one to use when working on large pieces of needlepoint.

Tent stitch

This stitch is always made in the same direction over one canvas intersection, and should be worked diagonally across the canvas, as this strengthens the work and prevents the canvas from being pulled out of shape. All of the needlepoint rugs shown in this book were worked in this stitch.

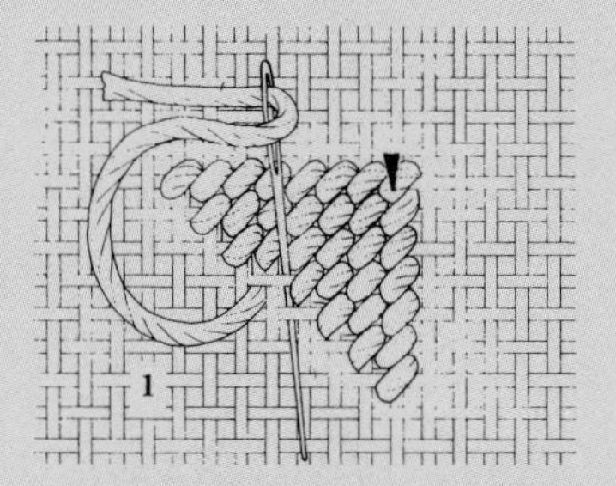

1 *Work diagonally, starting at top right. Bring needle out and take it up to right over 1 canvas intersection. Insert downwards under 2 horizontal threads and bring needle out ready to form the next stitch. Continue in this way to the end of the row.*

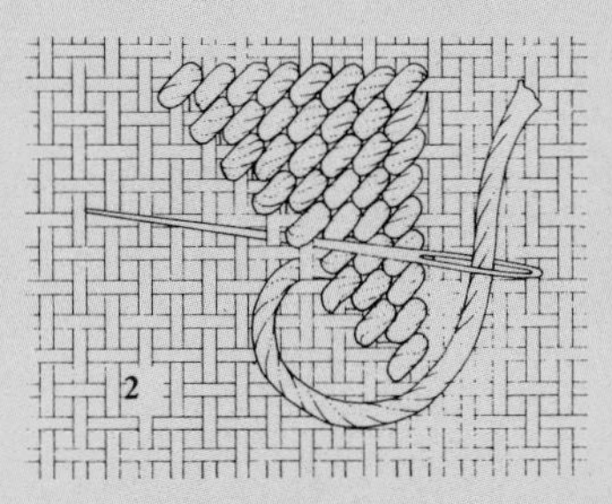

2 *On the return row work back up the line of stitches filling in the spaces left on the previous journey. Take needle up to right over 1 canvas intersection and insert it horizontally under 2 vertical threads. Bring needle out again ready to form the next stitch in the same way.*

BLOCKING AND SETTING

Blocking is the term given to smoothing the finished needlepoint or stretching it into shape. It is essential to take care over this since the final look of the work will depend on it being the correct shape and having an even finish.

Needlepoint is blocked face downwards. If the blocking is done correctly the needlepoint should not need ironing. However, should it be necessary, use a cool iron pressed lightly on to the work and lifted up and down, not rubbed across the surface, to ensure that the stitches are not flattened during the process.

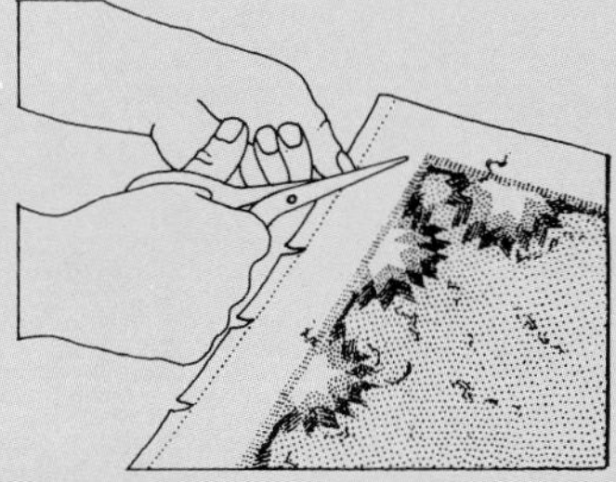

1 *First cover a clean soft board with plastic, put the paper marked with the correct outline on it and the needlepoint on top, placed face downwards. Snip the selvage so that the canvas will stretch evenly.*

2 *Lightly hammer a single tack into the canvas margin at the center top. Pull the canvas gently, making sure that the threads are at right angles to each other, and tack the center bottom. Repeat this process on the two sides.*

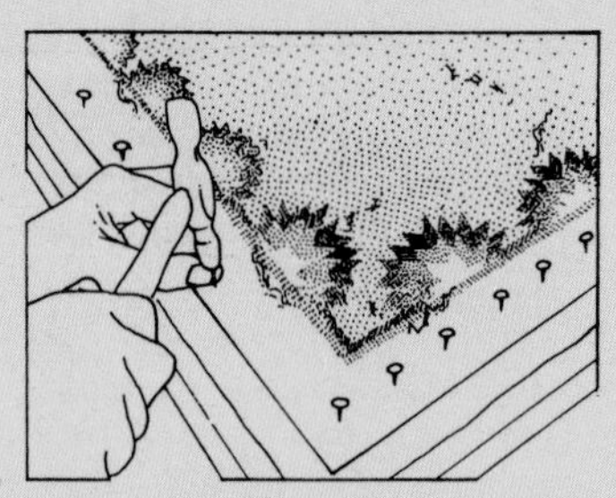

3 *Easing the needlepoint into the correct shape and working from the center towards the corner on all edges, lightly insert more tacks at 1in. intervals.*

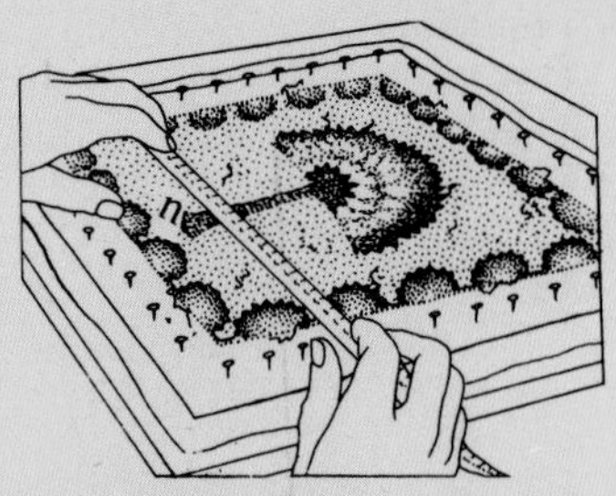

4 *Carefully measure and match canvas to correct shape, adjusting tacks where necessary. Dampen areas requiring a lot of stretching. Hammer tacks securely.*

Once the needlepoint has been stretched into its correct shape, it must be set while still nailed down. Sponge the back of work lightly with cold water. Leave it to dry at room temperature and out of direct sunlight. It is important not to remove the work from the board until it is bone dry or you may find that it will become distorted again.

JOINING

If you have worked your needlepoint in several sections, block each piece separately before joining them together.

How to join on the straight

1 *Fold back the unworked area of canvas on the edge of one piece of needlepoint. Lay it face upwards on top of the unworked area of the other piece, matching up the pattern and placing it as near as possible to the needlepoint stitches. Pin together and then baste in position. Remove the pins.*

2 *Using carpet thread, slip stitch along the join, making sure that a stitch is made into each mesh of the canvas. Pull tight without puckering the canvas. Remove the basting stitches.*

3 *Work over the seam and any part of the canvas which may show. Use matching needlepoint stitches in the correct pattern and color sequence and hold the folds of unworked canvas away from the back of the work so as not to stitch through a double thickness.*

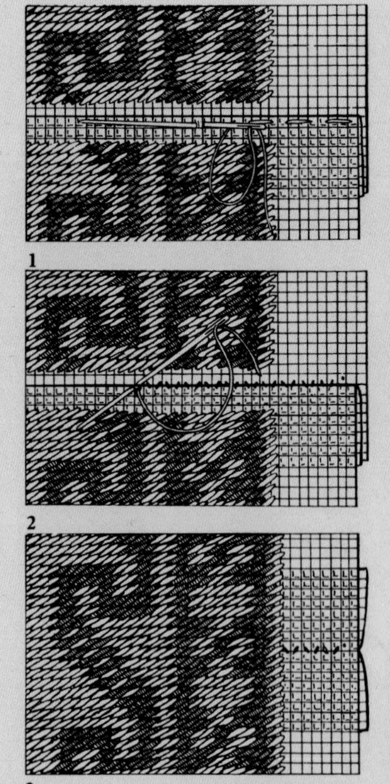

How to join on the diagonal

Lay the pieces on a flat surface, with the unworked canvas folded back, so that the diagonal edges meet to form a mitered corner. Join in the same way as above, taking care to work into each mesh and to match up the patten exactly.

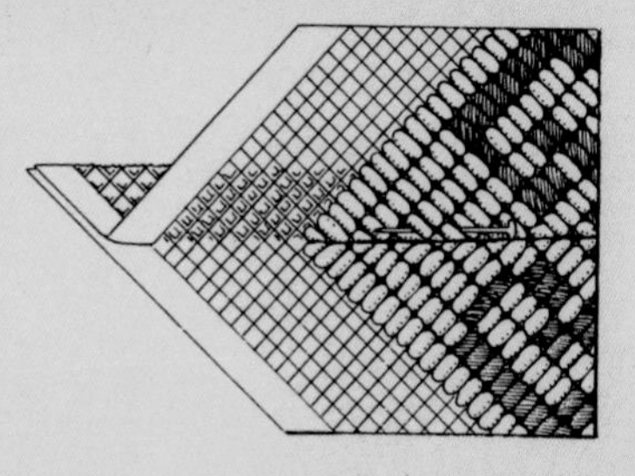

FINISHING

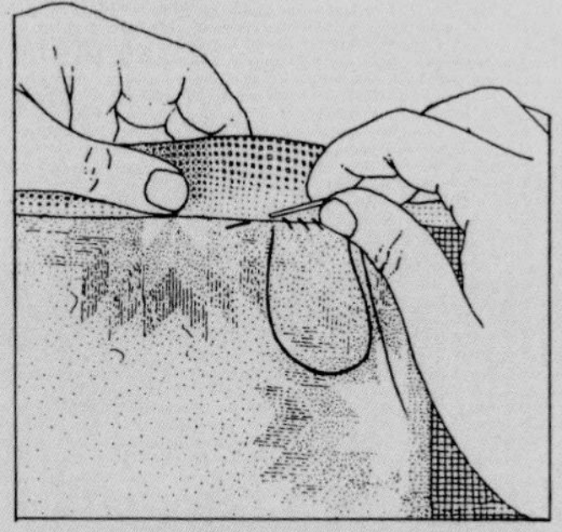

1 *Fold the unworked edges back. Slip stitch the edges down, using a sewing needle and strong carpet thread.*

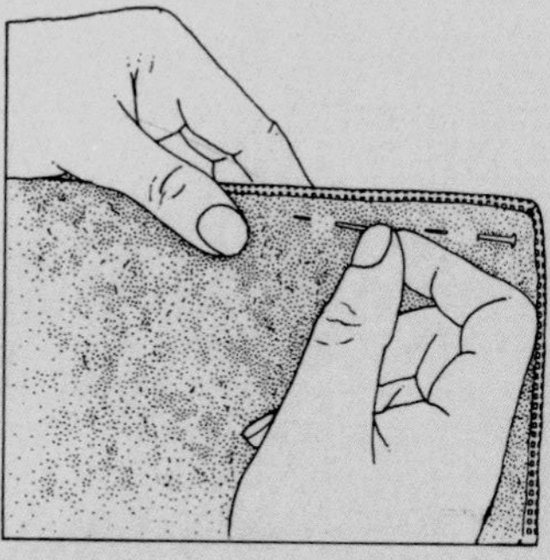

2 *Cut a piece of thin carpet felt the same size as the work. Pin it in position to the back of the tapestry, and slip stitch it into place.*

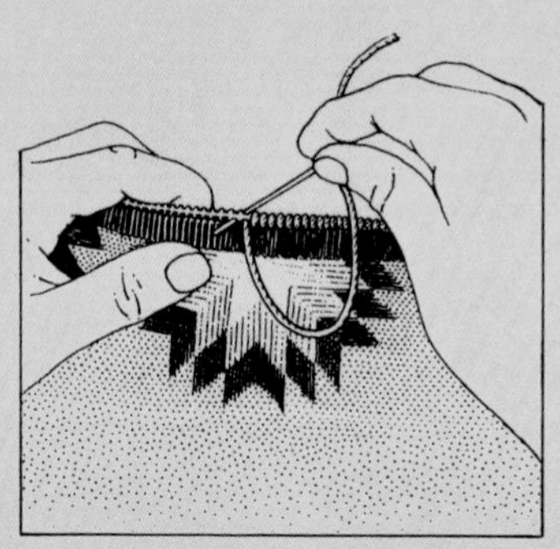

3 *Turn the tapestry face upwards, and finish by working matching needlepoint stitches along the edges to cover any exposed canvas threads.*

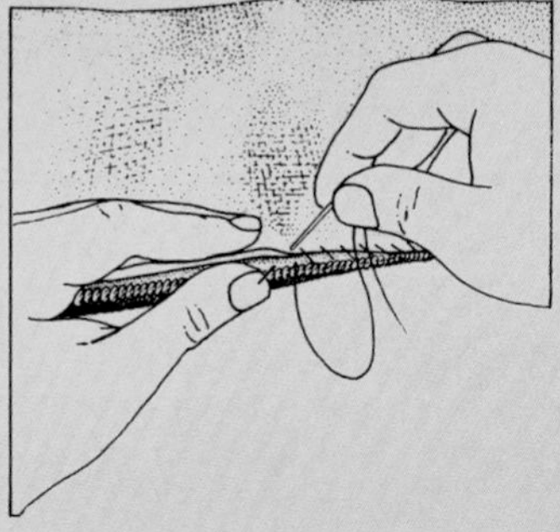

4 *Finally, cut a piece of burlap which is 2in. larger all around than the carpet or rug. Spread out the needlepoint with the felt lining face upwards and make certain that it is straight and even. Turn in the extra 2in. of the burlap and slip stitch it on to the back of the work.*

Braided rugs

EQUIPMENT
Fabric, scissors, sewing needle, heavy thread, safety pin, yardstick, chalk, lacers (or curved carpet needles) to join braids.

Fabric
As with rag rugs, braided rugs can use up leftover sewing scraps or torn strips from old clothes. Do not mix light- and heavy-weight fabrics, as the finished effect will be uneven and bumpy.

Estimating quantity
The quantity of fabric required depends upon several factors: the size of the rug, weight of the fabric, width of the strips, and tension of the braid. Generally, one to two feet of yardage is lost for every four feet that you braid. If you are making a continuous spiral, each round will take up about 7–8in. more than the previous one. A further 7in. will be needed for joining the ends.

Preparing the fabric
Any used materials should be washed and new ones should be pre-shrunk before braiding. The working strands are made by cutting the fabric into bias strips. These are usually 2–4in. wide, depending on the weight of the fabric. Cut heavy fabric narrower than light ones. It is helpful to use a yardstick and to mark cutting lines with chalk. Join strips together into 10- to 12-yard lengths.

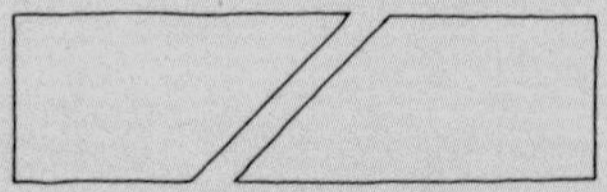

1 Strips cut on the diagonal

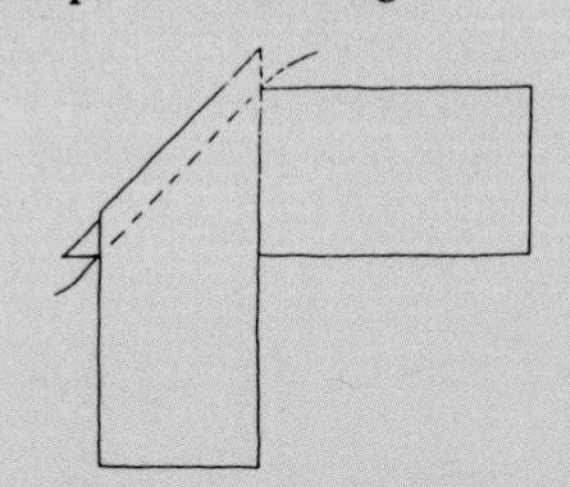

2 Stitching along the diagonal

Joining the strips
1 *Cut diagonally across the bias ~~on the~~ straight grain.*
2 *Place the 2 strips together, matching them up on the diagonal as shown. Stitch along the join.*
3 *Press seams open, trim off corners and unfold the pieces into a continuous length and trim off any surplus material.*

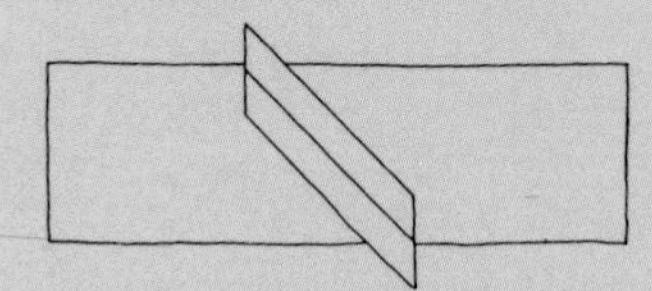

3 The opened-out join

Folding the strips
1 *Lay the strip out flat, right side downwards.*
2 *Fold the strip sides to middle as shown.*
3 *Fold in half again down the center line. Tack into place if you want to produce a round effect, or press lightly with an iron if you want the finished braid to look more flattened.*

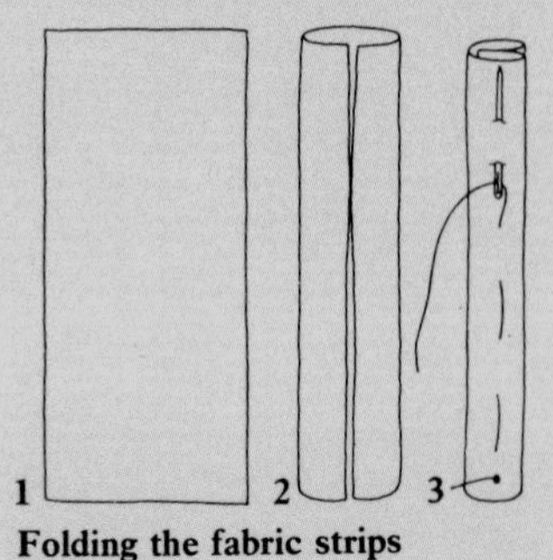

Folding the fabric strips

BEGINNING THE BRAID

The first thing to do is to secure the strands together at the top.

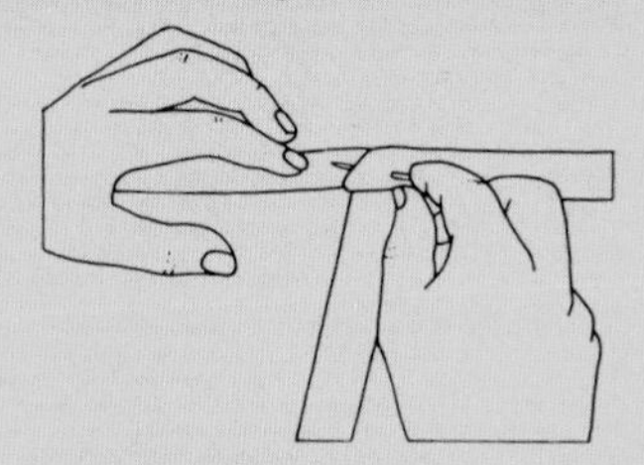

1 *For a 3-strand braid, join two strips together. Slot a third strip into the fold of the other two at the center. Secure with a pin or a few stitches.*

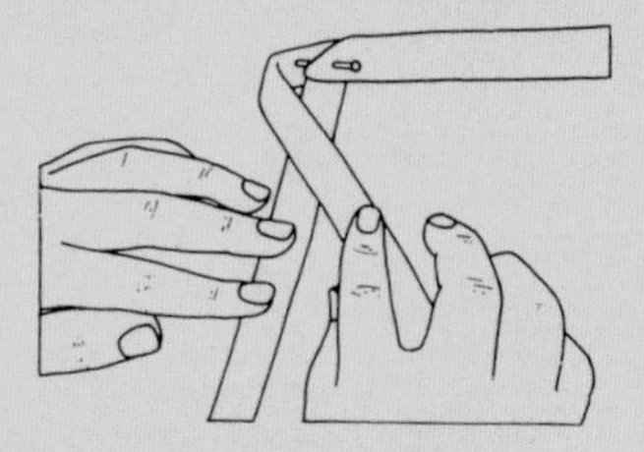

2 *Begin braiding as shown. The left half of the top strip becomes the first strand of the braid, the vertical strip the second, and the right half of the top strip the third.*

BRAIDING

By varying the technique slightly, it is possible to produce either a rounded or flattened effect on the finish braid. In both cases, it is essential to mount the tops of the strands firmly to the working surface before beginning the braiding.

How to make a rounded braid

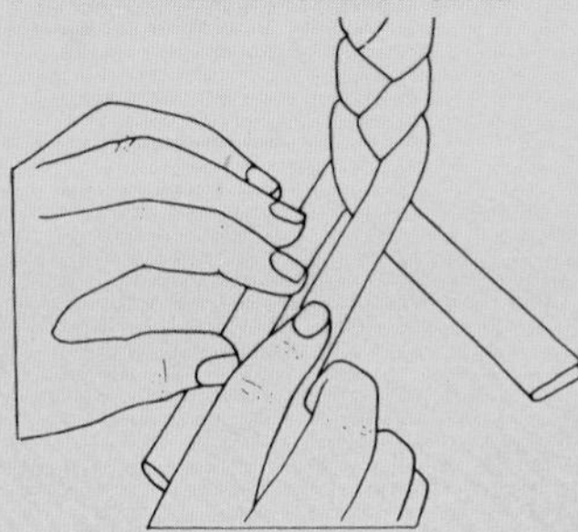

Work in the normal way, treating each strand as if it were a simple cord. Keep the open edges to the right throughout. To produce even fatter, rounder braids, make each strand bulkier by lining it with another strip of fabric before folding it over and beginning to braid.

How to make a flattened braid

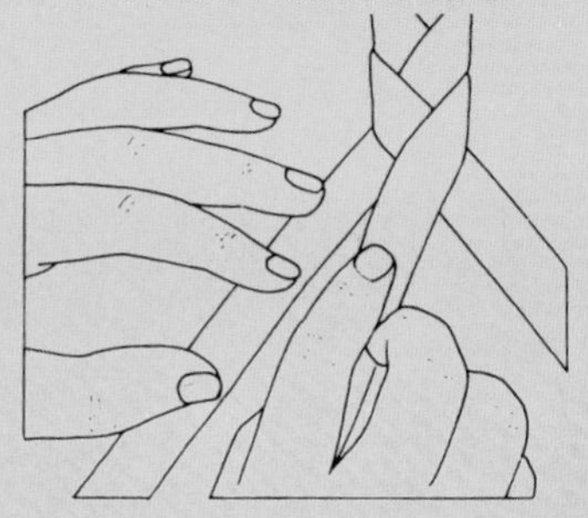

Work in the normal way, but this time fold the strands over in a sharp crease at the outer edges of the braid. Start off by setting the open edges of the fabric strands to the right, so that as the work progresses, the open edges always face up towards the top of the braid.

Finishing

When the braid has been worked to the required length, finish off by darning back and securing the ends.

Thread the ends of the strands back into the loops of the braid on the wrong side. Secure them by stitching over the ends, keeping the stitches out of sight.

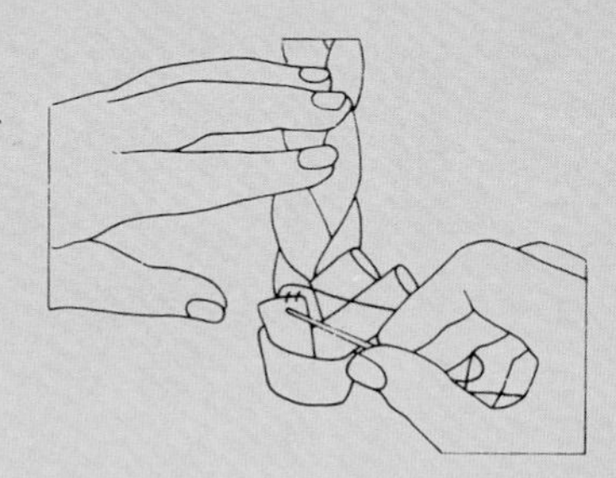

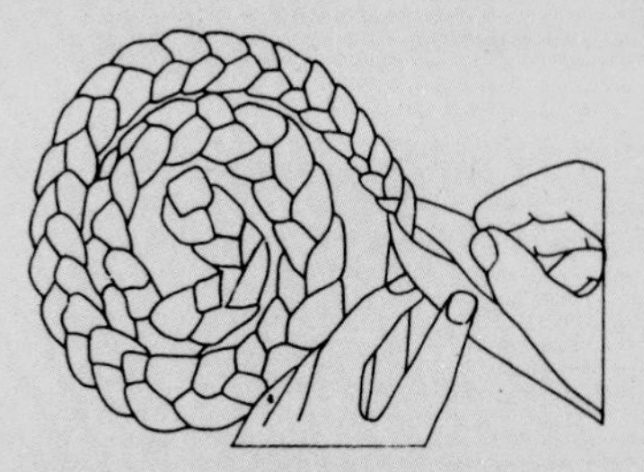

How to finish off a spiral
The neatest way to finish off a spiral is to taper the end of each strand before completing the braid. The braid will become thinner and thinner until it can be unobtrusively joined into the spiral.

Backing
Attaching a backing will make the braided rug more hard-wearing. Use a burlap backing. Either cut out a piece slightly smaller than the rug and stick it in place with carpet tape, or cut out a piece slightly larger than the rug, turn the edges under and stitch it in place.

Simple woven rugs

Weaving is simply the interlacing of two separate sets of threads at right angles to each other. A frame holds the vertical threads ('warp') taut, and a horizontal set of threads ('weft') is woven backwards and forwards between them. Although various types of weaves can be worked on cards, frames or looms, this book focuses on the tapestry weave made on a simple frame.

EQUIPMENT

Frame
The frame you use may be a canvas-stretching frame, a sturdy old picture frame, even an old bed frame. It is important to work with a very strong frame (hard wood is the best) which cannot bend out of shape. To discover what size frame you'll need, add 6in. (3in. to top and bottom) to the height of the tapestry you wish to weave and 2in. (1in. to each side) to the width. These measurements are the minimum inside measurements required for the frame. Some weavers prefer to wrap the warp threads around the ends of a frame in a figure-of-8 fashion, eliminating the use of nails, as this enables them to weave many different types (weights and thicknesses) of rugs using the same frame.

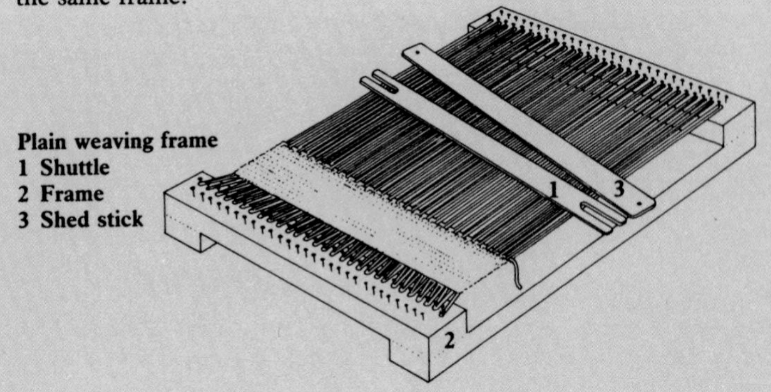

Plain weaving frame
1 Shuttle
2 Frame
3 Shed stick

Shed stick
The shed is the space between the alternating warp threads through which the weft yarn is passed, but it is not obvious when using the simple frame shown in the following illustrations. The shed stick separates the alternate warps to create that space.

Shuttle
This is a flat stick, preferably the same length as the width of the warp, with a notch cut at both ends. It brings the weft yarn through the shed.

Yarns
Warp yarns must be strong, as they are held permanently under tension, and they must also be smooth, since they take a lot of abuse. If a warp yarn is at all hairy it will stick to the other warp yarns and will be difficult to separate.

Weft yarns can be made of anything that is reasonably pliable. It does not even have to be a yarn, but can be cord, raffia, cane, plastic or paper, depending on what you want your finished fabric to be.

PREPARING THE WARP

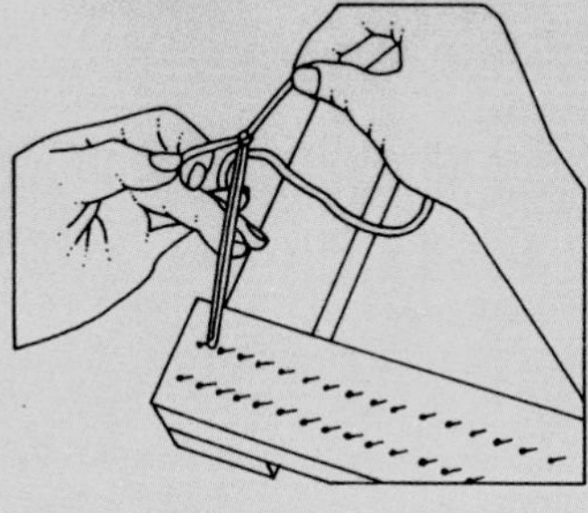

1 *Fasten the first thread by securely tying one end of warp yarn to first nail (bottom left).*

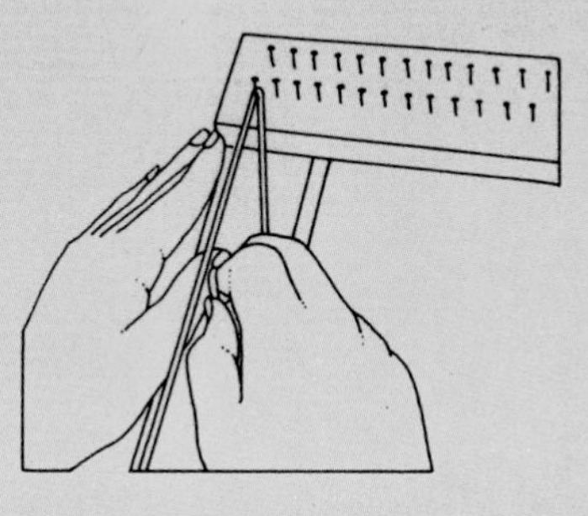

2 *Wrap the warp yarn around the opposite nail (top left) from left to right.*

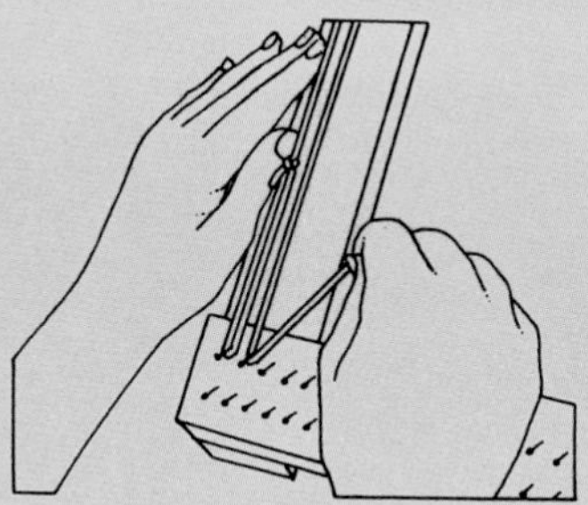

3 *Pass yarn around 2nd nail (bottom left) from left to right. Continue across width of frame, checking that the tension is even.*

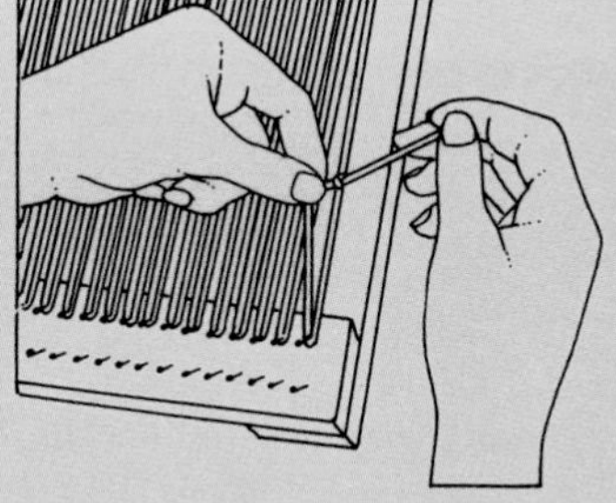

4 *Finish by fastening yarn to last nail, fairly near bottom.*

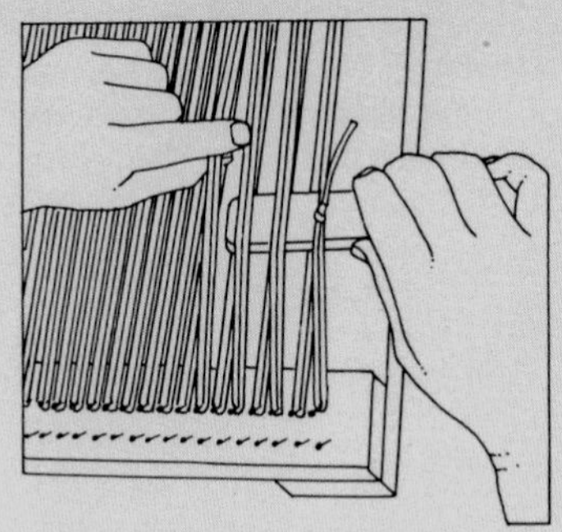

5 *Weave in shed stick from right to left, passing it over one* **pair** *of threads, and under next, alternately.*

Using a finer warp

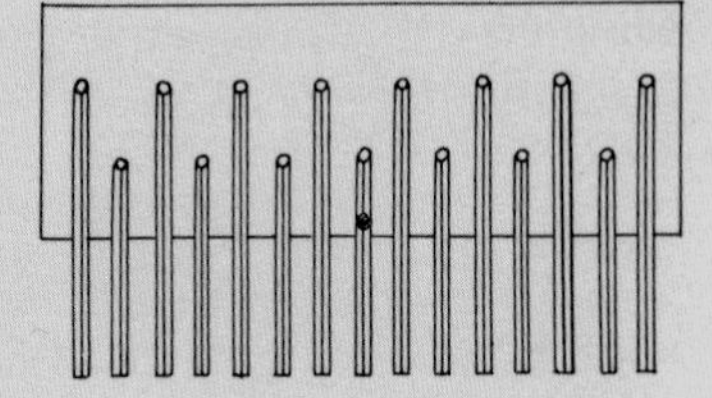

To achieve a finer warp with more threads to the inch you must use both rows of nails. Wind the yarn first around the two inner rows, then the two outer rows so that all four rows are covered.

STARTING TO WEAVE

The weft threads are woven in from right and left. Different textures of fabric can be woven by using varying thicknesses of warp and weft threads as required, and changing the positioning of the shed stick.

1 *Turn shed stick on its side and pass shuttle from left and right through shed, leaving about 2–3in. of weft yarn loose on the left side of the warp.*

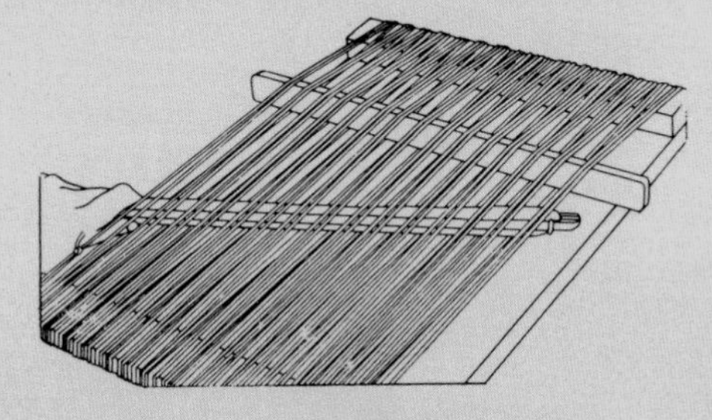

2 *Turn shed stick back to its original position and use it to push your first weft thread into place at front of frame. Insert next weft thread by darning shuttle in and out of the alternate warp threads from right and left.*

3 *Push 2nd weft thread into place with shed stick. A dinner fork is sometimes preferred for beating back the weft.*

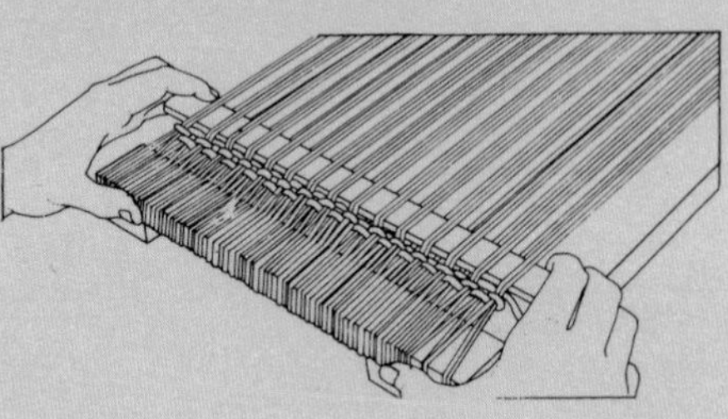

4 *Continue in the same way, repeating the process from Step 1.*

FINISHING OFF

Remove the work from the frame by unhooking it or by cutting the warp yarn at each end.

Then thread each loose strand of yarn through needle. Push needle down into fabric, drawing yarn through with it. Pull needle out, leaving loose strand hidden in fabric.

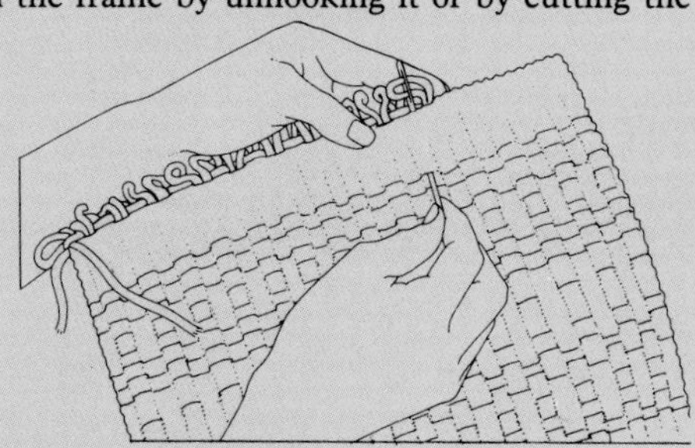

INTRODUCING A NEW COLOR

A new color can be added at any point by adding a new weft thread with a second shuttle, ensuring that the color wefts are interlocked at the edges. This will make the edges tidier and the weaving easier.

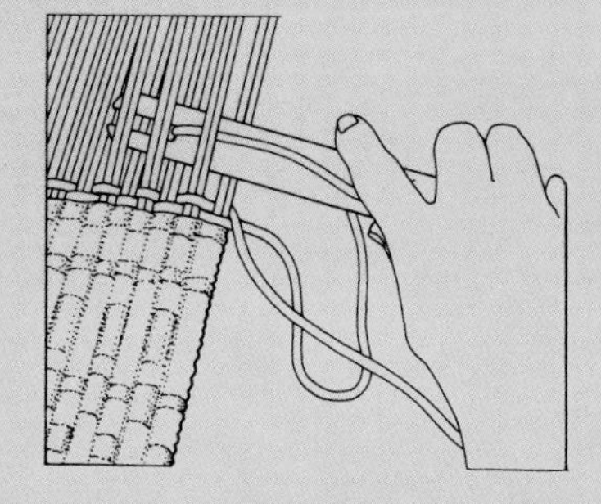

Weaving a second color

First weft is passed under second weft at edge before weaving first color back into warp.

FLORALS

Floral patterns are among the most popular motifs used by rug makers. They make up into extremely decorative rugs and wall hangings, as well as cushions and seat covers. In the creation of traditional or modern floral designs, a light or dark background will make the individual flowers stand out best.

Petite rose

Hand hooked cushion cover This dainty cushion cover was designed to match the rosy rug on the facing page.

Rosy window

Hand hooked rug A stained-glass window was the inspiration for this design.

Materials Brushed wool fabrics; finer wool for the black lines.

Construction First, outline the flowers and squares using black strips. Then fill in the rest at random, though bear in mind that it is always easier to start in the middle and work outwards.

Fleur deco

Hand hooked rug 1920's Neat symmetrical pattern in contrasting lights and darks gives this rug a bold but simple look.

Materials Wool strips, dyed if necessary to required shades.

Construction This simple design can be easily planned out on graph paper. Hand hook, starting at centers of flowers, and work outwards. Follow with the outlines and borders, then fill in the background. Alternate light and dark shades of one color in the border triangles.

Lilies

Needlepoint rug This peach-colored rug was designed in Art Nouveau style with a pleasing balanced look.

Materials Persian wool on single canvas, 10 stitches/in.

Construction Use tent stitch, p. 15. This rug is so nicely symmetrical that you need only to draw half of it on graph paper to use as a guide for the entire piece.

Mille fleurs

Punch hooked rug This cheerful collection of flowers and leaves was constructed with leftover scraps of different colored yarns.

Materials For flowers, scraps of 2-ply yarns in any colors that look well together; 2-ply yarn for background; 7 ounces (200g) of yarn are used up per square foot (30cm × 30cm).

Construction Work the flowers, stems and leaves first using a ¼-in (½-cm) loop. Then work the border. Outline the flowers, stems and leaves in the background shade, then fill in the rest of the background.

Fruit and flowers

Needlepoint rug A richly designed rug as appealing as an orchard in full flower.

Materials Single canvas, 16 stiches/in., or double canvas 10 stitches/in., as these come in 60in. widths; crewel wool.

Construction Use tent stitch. Start in the middle of the canvas and work outwards. When complete, cut canvas to round shape, leaving 5 – 6 in. (13 – 15cm) all around. Turn back the hem, cutting slits where necessary to allow the rug to lay flat. Finish as described in Basic Techniques, p. 17.

Experiment on paper first by sketching fruit and shading in areas with colored pencils or crayons. The appearance of shiny, ripe fruit or glimmering sunlight falling across a leaf can make your work come alive. Try three or four gradations of one color, changing from dark to light to bright, then dark again. A very dark background color also will enhance the richness of the design.

Detail Represents 25% of the rug.

Strawberries and blueberries

Hand hooked rug depicting two of America's favorite summer fruits.

Materials Wool strips, burlap backing.

Construction Hook small details first, then the rest at random, filling in the background last. Since blueberries are in groups of three, four and five, take care to separate them visually by outlining them and hooking each individually in semi-circular patterns. Try to keep the points of their "stars" sharp.

Special note There is no one right way to hand hook. Everyone develops his/her own style, and the height of the loops hooked may vary from person to person. Simply practice to see what feels right for you. An average height of loops for very narrow strips is ⅛in. (¼cm). However, the wider the strip of wool used, the higher the loop will be, and the more meshes of canvas should be skipped between loops so that they are not packed together too tightly.

Detail Represents 23% of the rug.

Rhododendrons

Needlepoint rug This vibrant collection of flowers was based on different varieties of living rhododendrons.

Materials Single canvas, 3 stitches/in.; tapestry wool.

Construction It is advisable to draw your design on graph paper, especially if it is complex. Work individual squares in tent stitch, and join together (after blocking and setting). The corners of each square contain one-quarter of a rondel, which is formed when four pieces are put together.

Detail Represents 10% of the rug.

NATURE

The scope for designing rugs inspired by nature is delightfully unlimited. By using a variety of textured yarn or wool throughout a design, you can achieve the effect of wheat growing in a field, prickles standing out on a cactus, or clouds passing through the sky. The wild look of a rushing waterfall or the precise detail of the smallest butterfly wing can be accurately captured by careful use of yarn. Rugs depicting natural subjects in any technique give magnificent results.

Sunburst

Victorian hand hooked rug, probably used as a hearth rug. The sun's rays emanating outwards mimicked the warmth of the fire doing the same.

Autumn landscape

Hand hooked wall hanging (framed) This impressionistic wall hanging is extremely rich in color and texture.

Materials Tie-dyed silk strips for the sky, wool for the hills, thick knitting yarns for the fields; blunt-ended needle for flat work.

Construction Outline the shape of the hills where they meet the sky. Work sky, wooded hills, then downwards until complete. As a variation of texture and technique, sew flat long-and-short stitches to suggest wheat fields. Use reverse hooking (hooking with the right side facing you) to achieve another texture.

Butterflies

Needlepoint rug based on authentic butterflies and full of color and vitality.

Materials Single canvas, 8 stitches/in.; crewel wool.

Construction Use tent stitch. Any small detail should be worked first, then the background. Here the background has been worked using different shades of one color to achieve a subtle effect. Refer to nature books for accurate pictures of the shape and coloring of animals' and insects' anatomies.

Detail Represents 12% of the rug.

Garden path

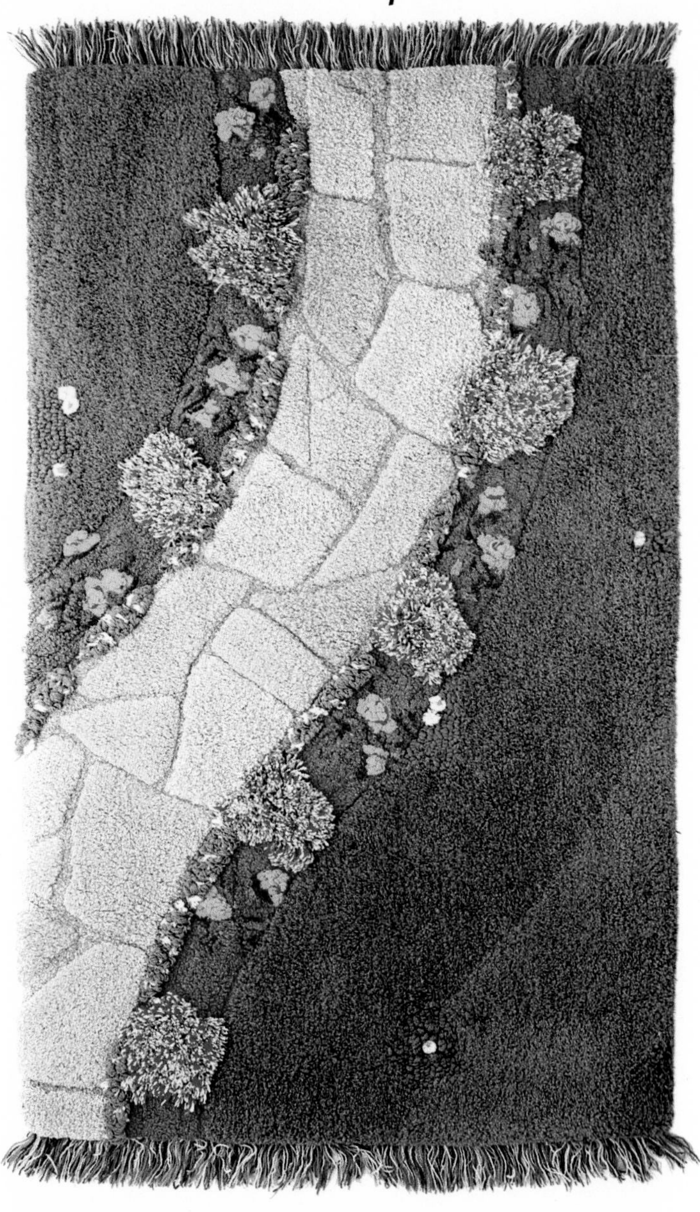

Latch hooked rug A truly life-like piece of nature that stays in bloom all year long.

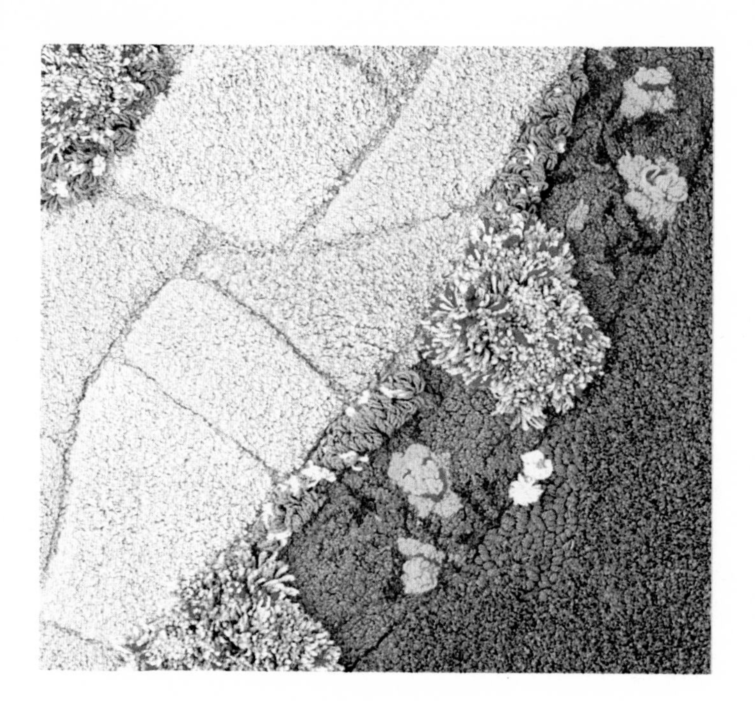

Materials Three strands of 2-ply yarn used at the same time (in each hooked space); latch hook canvas.

Construction For the grass: use three strands of fine wool in light green, vibrant green and darker green. For the stones: vary the shades slightly to achieve different-color stones. To obtain a 3-dimensional effect, trim short the yarns that form the "cement" around the stones. The lobelia flowers were worked in an uneven stitch (instead of bringing equal lengths of the piece of yarn through the hole, keep one end shorter than the other). This gives them a shaggy look. (Threads can also be trimmed unevenly after hooking.)
For the daisies: make a pom-pom. Flatten out and use a darning stitch with yellow yarn to sew the center of the flower. Make sure that the flattened shape is maintained and that all the threads are secure. Wind a green thread around the darning thread to make the stem. Then sew the ends into the rug. When the rug is completed, fringe the edges and apply a backing.

Detail Represents 12% of the rug.

By a waterfall

Hand hooked wall hanging convincingly depicting a fast-flowing waterfall.

Materials Organdy, tie-dyed silk, netting, thick knitting wools, coatings, angora, mohair and lurex were all used here.

Construction Roughly outline the shape of the waterfall on the backing and also the shape of the cliffs where they meet the sky. Work the waterfall in shallow loops, then the sky in longer loops. Hook the cliffs to the same height as the sky, working from the waterfall out to the edges.

Desert flower

Latch hooked wall hanging A 3-dimensional cactus wall hanging which proves gentle to the touch.

Materials Fine and fluffy yarns; latch hook canvas.

Construction Latch hook the pot and body of the cactus in shallow-to-medium height tufts using fine wool three strands at a time. Prickles are simply long strands left sticking out; smaller prickles are uneven tufts (as in Garden path, p. 41). To finish, cut around the shape of the cactus, leaving 5 – 6 in. (13 – 15cm) to turn back. Glue hem to back of canvas, cutting canvas where necessary to keep it flat. Back with strong cloth if using as a rug.

GEOMETRICS

Diamonds, squares, triangles — any angles, in fact, are easy shapes to imitate in just about any rug technique. Many early American rug makers borrowed the repeating block patterns of patchwork quilts in designing their own hooked rugs. Some of these are included in this section.

Composition on black

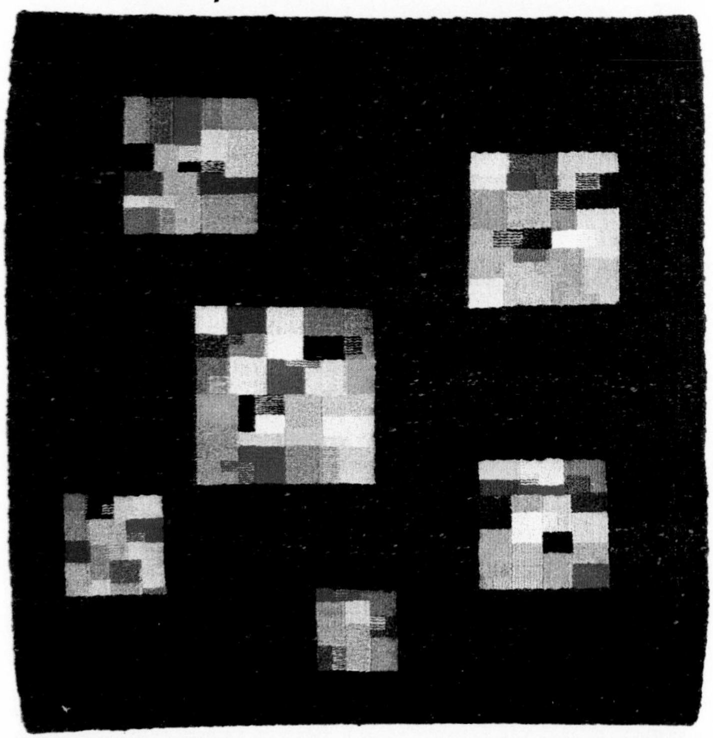

Woven wall hanging showing different-sized windows of striking colors.

Materials Dark brown cotton for the warp, black handspun wool for the weft.

Construction Tapestry weave in small vertical slits. For windows, dovetailing and hatching are used to create the juxtaposition of color.

When two woven areas meet vertically, a slit is formed.

Dovetailing breaks the vertical line of separate sections into a zig-zag.

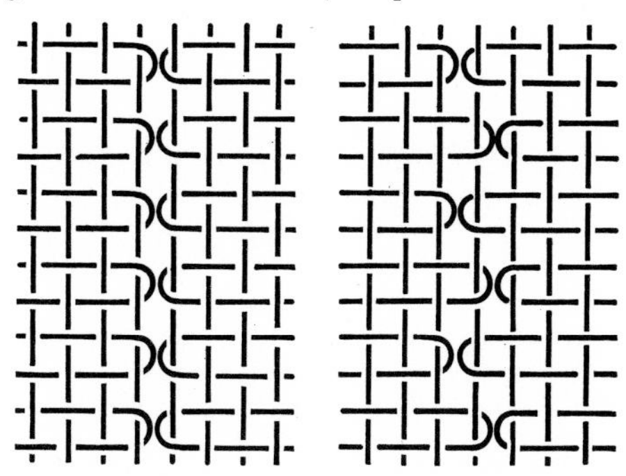

Hatching, a "meet and separate" weave, can create an interesting effect. First take the weft of one color across into another area of color and leave it at the front of the weaving. Bring the second color weft in from the opposite selvage until it meets the first, and leave this second yarn at the front. Change the shed and separate the colors by weaving them back to the edges. Continue in this way, varying the points where the two colors meet.

In hatching, two weft threads started from opposite sides of the weave meet and separate.

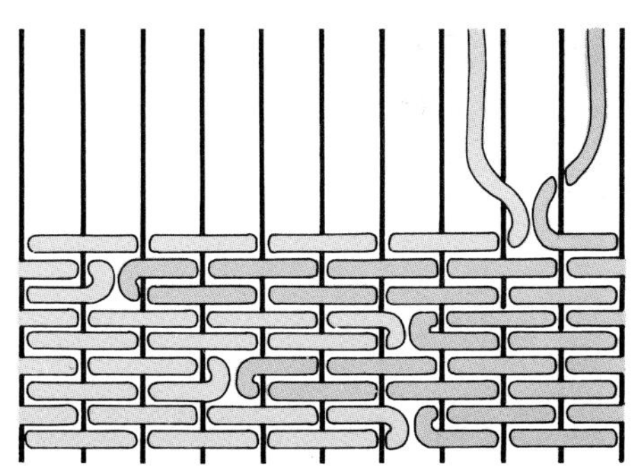

Between the lines

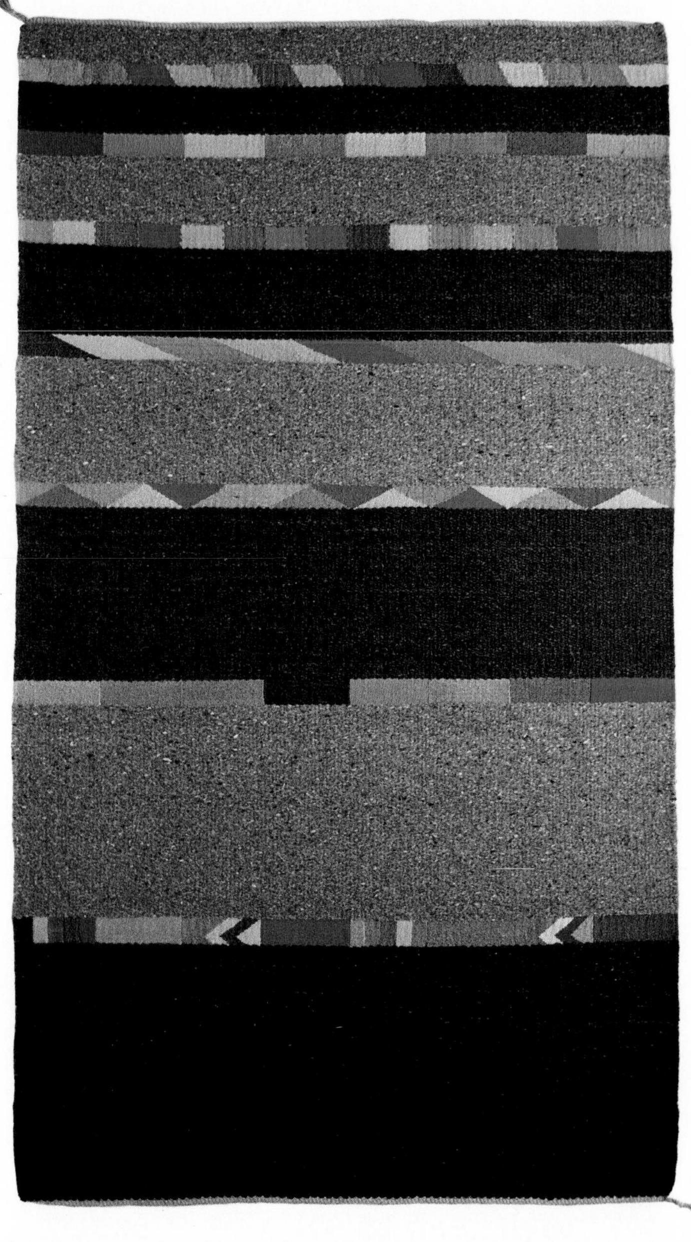

Woven rug inspired by Navajo Indian designs, in rich earthy tones.

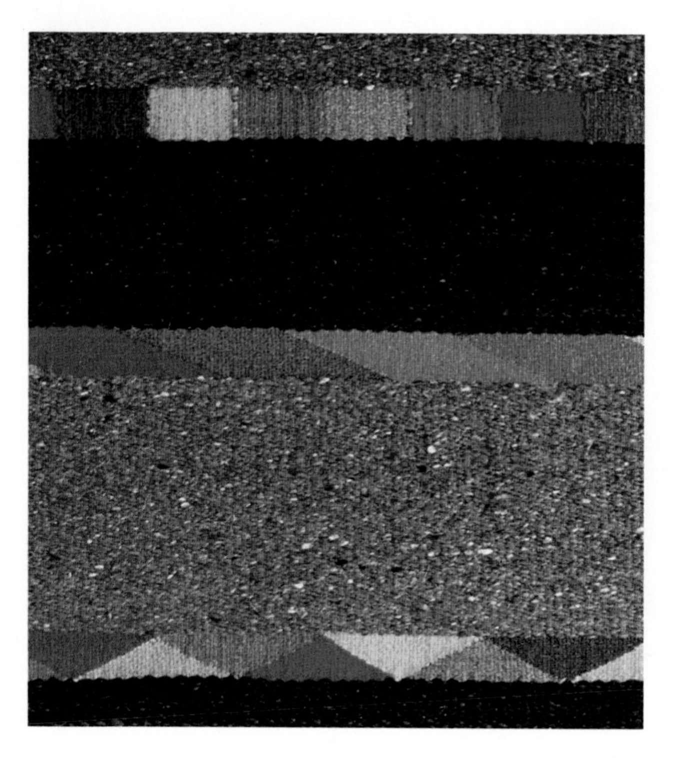

Materials Berber yarns; linen warp.

Construction Use tapestry weave, worked in decreasing stripes, to give a feeling of perspective. Use smaller shapes (triangles and squares), joining them together by hatching (see p. 45). To form triangles, gradually decrease the number of warp ends being woven on each side of the triangle. Weave 2 or 3 rows across the bottom of the shape, then weave subsequent rows, decreasing warp ends each row. By decreasing two or three warp ends at a time, a more gradual slope will be created. Work to peak of triangle. Reverse for "upside-down" triangle by starting with peak and increasing number of warp ends woven.

Detail Represents 14% of the rug.

Criss-cross squares

Late nineteenth century American hand hooked rug whose design was undoubtedly taken from popular patchwork quilt patterns.

Draw one square on graph paper as a guide. Hook a cross over each square, and working from the center outwards, fill in the stripes for each triangle of the square. Try alternating stripes with light and dark colors, or with different shades of the same color. A repeating color pattern can give a neat uniform look to the completed rug, but fine results can also be obtained by choosing colors randomly.

Log cabin

Late nineteenth century American hand hooked rug adapted from the traditional patchwork quilt pattern.

Draw one square of pattern on graph paper to determine sizes of "corners" within the square. Divide canvas into equal squares. Work small lower left "box", then outer corners until square is filled. Go to the next square, and either repeat using the same color pattern, or devise a new color pattern. Log cabin is often worked with lighter colors in the lower corner of each square with progressively darker corners built around them to the upper right corner.

Florametric

Late nineteenth century American hand hooked rug is a successful combination of traditional floral designs and patchwork quilt geometrics.

It will help to draw the design out first on graph paper. Draw large diamonds onto the backing, leaving equal spacing between them. Work floral patterns first. For the space between the large diamonds, either follow the design here for small triangles, or substitute your own design – perhaps stripes or simply a plain background.

Detail Represents 20% of the rug.

Starstruck

Early twentieth century American hand hooked rug reminiscent of patchwork quilt designs.

Materials Wool strips, burlap backing.

Construction Draw out one square to size on graph paper and follow this pattern repeatedly throughout. It will help to sketch out a small colored drawing of the entire rug as a guide. Divide your canvas into four equal horizontal rows. Work border and lines across to form rows, then work squares, changing colors where necessary.

Detail Represents 25% of the rug.

Four small "stars" in each square form a neat and pleasing pattern.

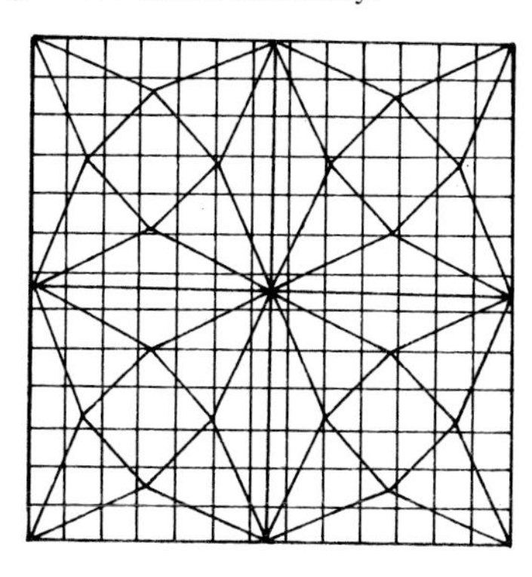

Deco diamond

Hand hooked rug 1920's A simple but elegant design in subtle shades exemplifying Art Deco style.

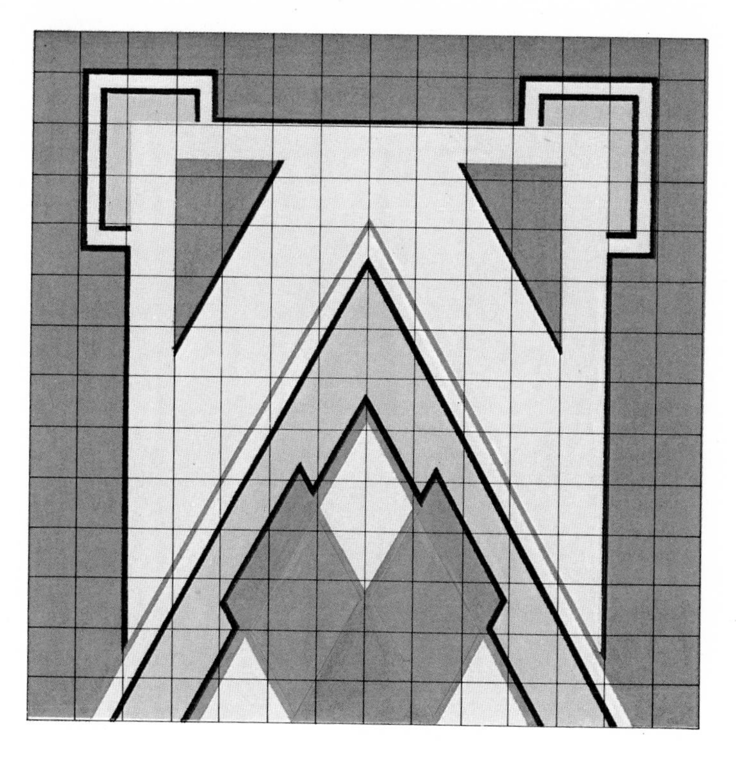

Materials Wool strips.

Construction This is a simple geometric design and one that is easy to plan out on graph paper. Experiment with different color combinations to find the effect that pleases you.

Crazy squares

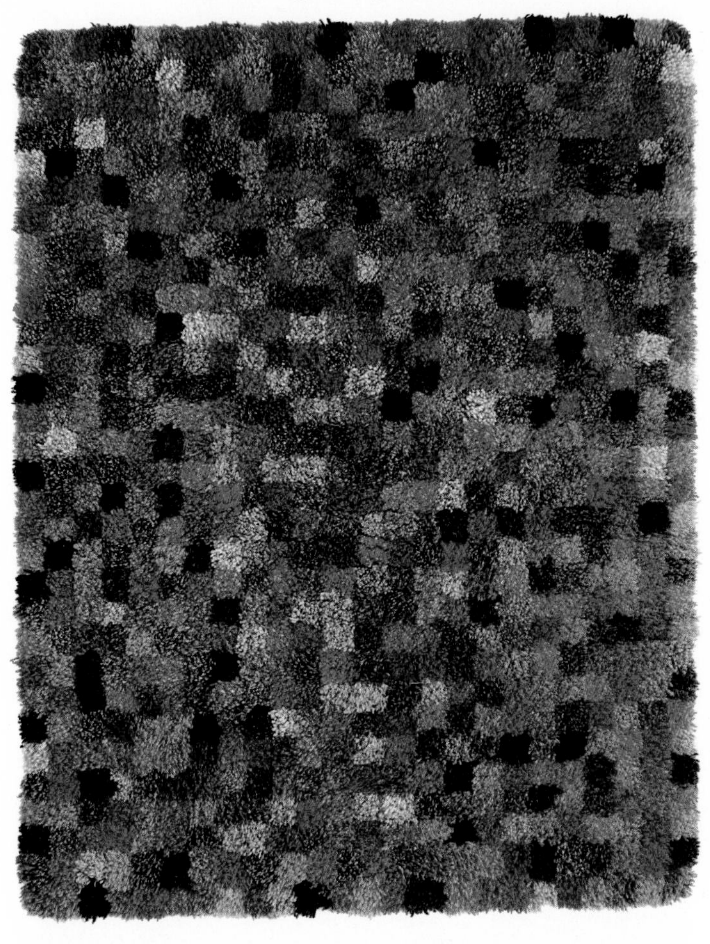

Latch hooked rug An easy-to-make project relying on color for its effects. Divide canvas into squares of equal size and hook, choosing colors at random. The repetition of individual colors gives the finished rug a sense of unity and movement.

Cave drawing

Latch hooked rug in a very basic and symmetrical, yet unusual, design. Pick an existing symbol, or make up your own and let your friends speculate upon its meaning.

ABSTRACTS

Unconnected images such as casual doodles or randomly placed geometrical objects such as dominoes falling through space make effective free-style rug designs. You are only limited by your imagination.

DJ's delight

Hand hooked rug of the 1980's reminiscent of the 1950's. Start in the middle and hook outwards in a circular pattern. When complete, cut shape out of canvas, leaving 5 – 6 inches (13 – 15cm) around. Turn edges to wrong side and glue to back. Glue entire area of rug.

Hide

Woven wall hanging One of the more complex examples of the pictorial weaves, this wall hanging illustrates the wide scope of designs possible using this technique.

Materials Rug wools on linen warp.

Construction The designer made small sketches of the rooms, then fitted them together as she wove up from the bottom. The windows are all the same; the light shade in them suggests sunlight. Where vertical lines (slits) occur, two sections were sewn together.

Windy day

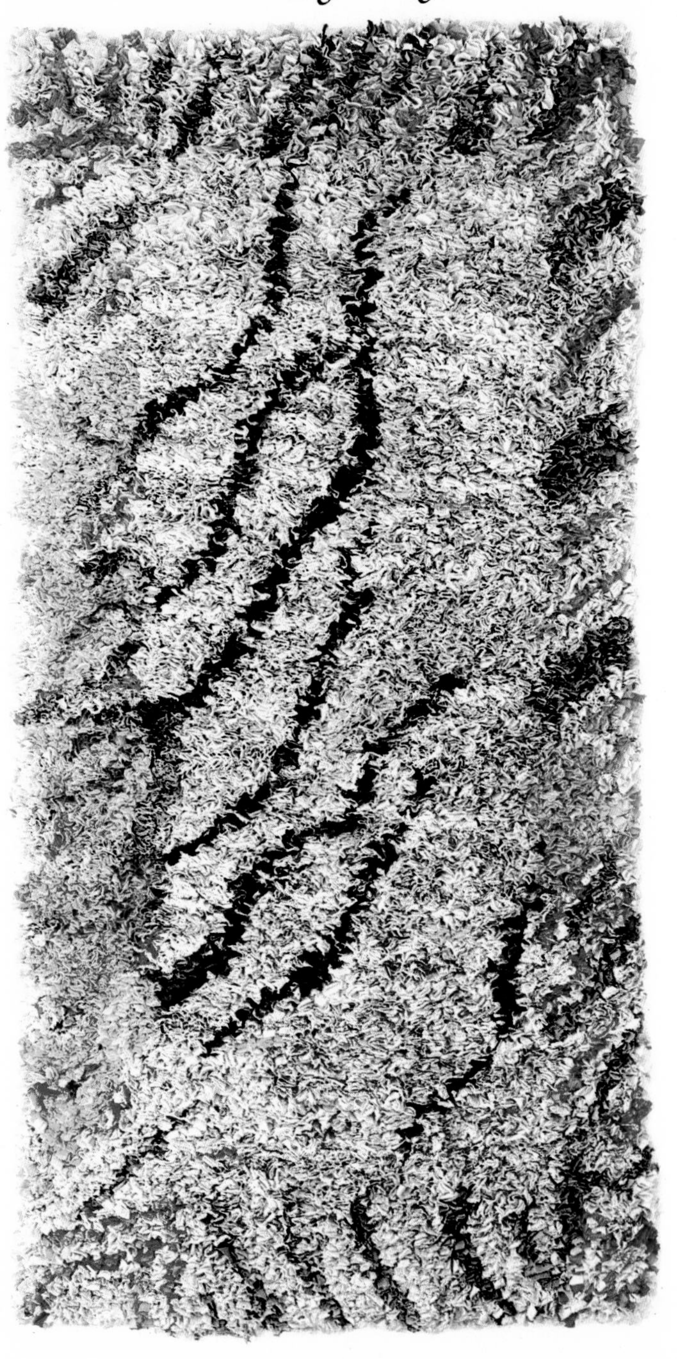

This Welsh prodded mat made in 1890 was probably recycled from a man's worn out work clothes and a woman's old winter coat.

The modern prodded rag rug (opposite) is a new interpretation of an old country craft.

Materials The designer of *Windy day* prefers cottons and silks, but any synthetic or natural fabric can be used. To increase the selection of colors, you can overdye the existing fabrics with any suitable household dye. Use coarse burlap for backing.

Construction Sketch the design on paper, then draw on the wrong side of the backing, keeping in mind that the sketch will be reversed in the finished rug, as the rug is prodded wrong side up. Also note that small detail is lost in the shaggy texture, so large or abstract patterns are best.
Work bold areas of color first, then fill in the background with mixed lighter colors.

Missing links

Punch hooked rug of neat shapes cleverly creates an optical illusion.

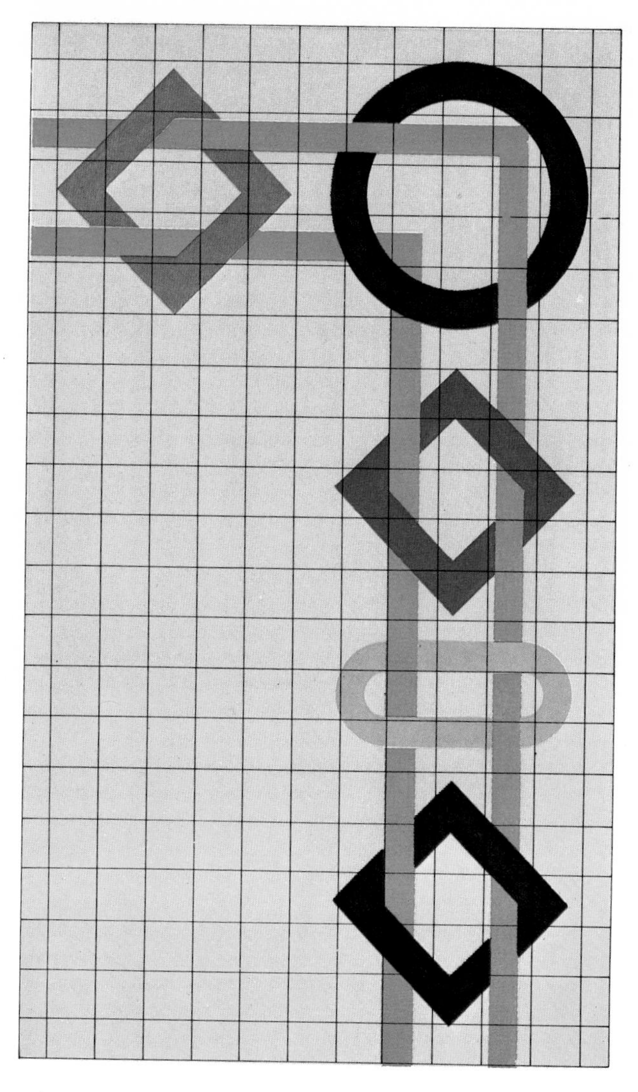

Materials 2-ply yarns in ¼-in. (½-cm) loops. Leftover yarns can be put to good use here.

Construction Draw the design on graph paper. Work the shapes first, then the connecting lines. Then fill in the spaces between the shapes and lines. Finally, outline the edge of the rug and the shapes and fill in the background.

Parallelogram

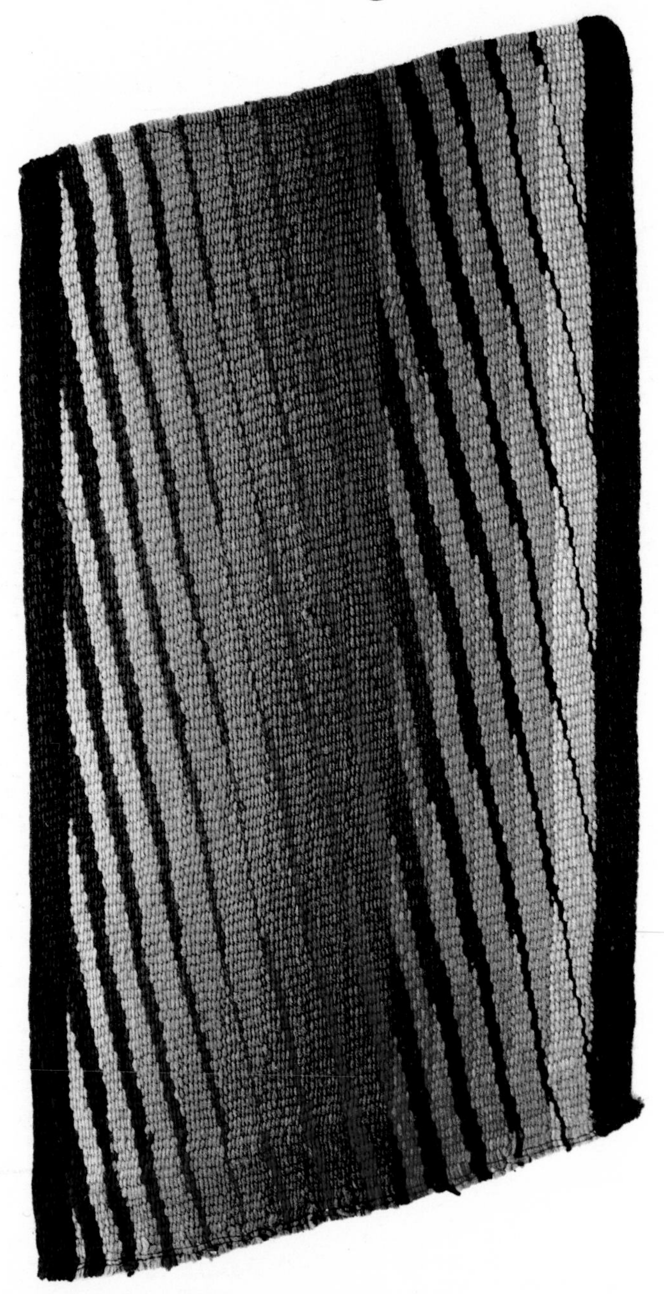

Braided wall hanging based on a woven technique usually attributed to North American Indian designs.

Materials Berber yarns (2-ply yarn for a finer texture wall hanging); wooden clamp. Make clamp with two pieces of wood ½in. (1cm) thick × 2in. (5cm) wide, cut 6in. (15cm) longer than the finished rug.

Construction First make up a small sample braid to determine your weaving tension and to indicate how many braids will make the hanging to the required width. Always work with an even number of threads in each braid. Cut lengths of yarn 2½ times the length of the finished work.

Clamp the cut lengths of yarn (the warp) between the two pieces of wood halfway along the length of the warp. The hanging is made in two parts: first braid one half from the clamp to the end, then reclamp onto the braided work, turn the whole piece around, and braid from the clamp to the other end.

To work:

1. Pick up the alternate warps of one braid, so that the first warp rises to an upper position and the second is dropped to a lower position.

2. The first upper thread is a weft thread and is pulled through the shed created.

3. Do the same with the second braid, but before bringing the first upper weft through, interlink it with the weft of the first braid.

4. The interlinking carries through until the last braid – the last weft comes out of the selvage and rests over the clamp.

5. Go back to the left-hand edge of the hanging and pick up the first loose thread. This is the next weft. Change the shed. Repeat steps 2 – 4, but when the last weft comes through the selvage, bring the first weft (which has been resting on the clamp) down under the second. Rest second weft over the clamp.

6. Continue in this way until you reach the desired length. To finish, bring the last weft back through the shed of the previous row in the opposite direction (right to left). Insert a strip of iron-on interfacing in the final shed, between the upper and lower warps. Then machine-stitch across. Wrap and tassel the remaining threads, or cut them straight across to 1 – 2in. (2.5 – 5 cm) from stitching, turn them under and sew to back. The top end can be turned under and sewn around a rod for hanging.

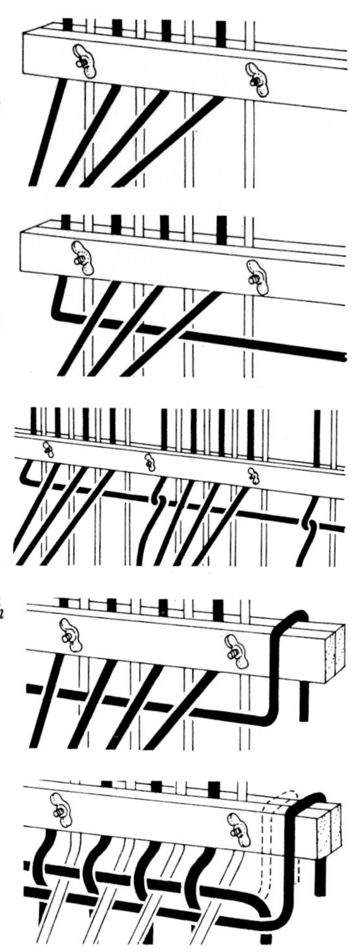

Harlequin

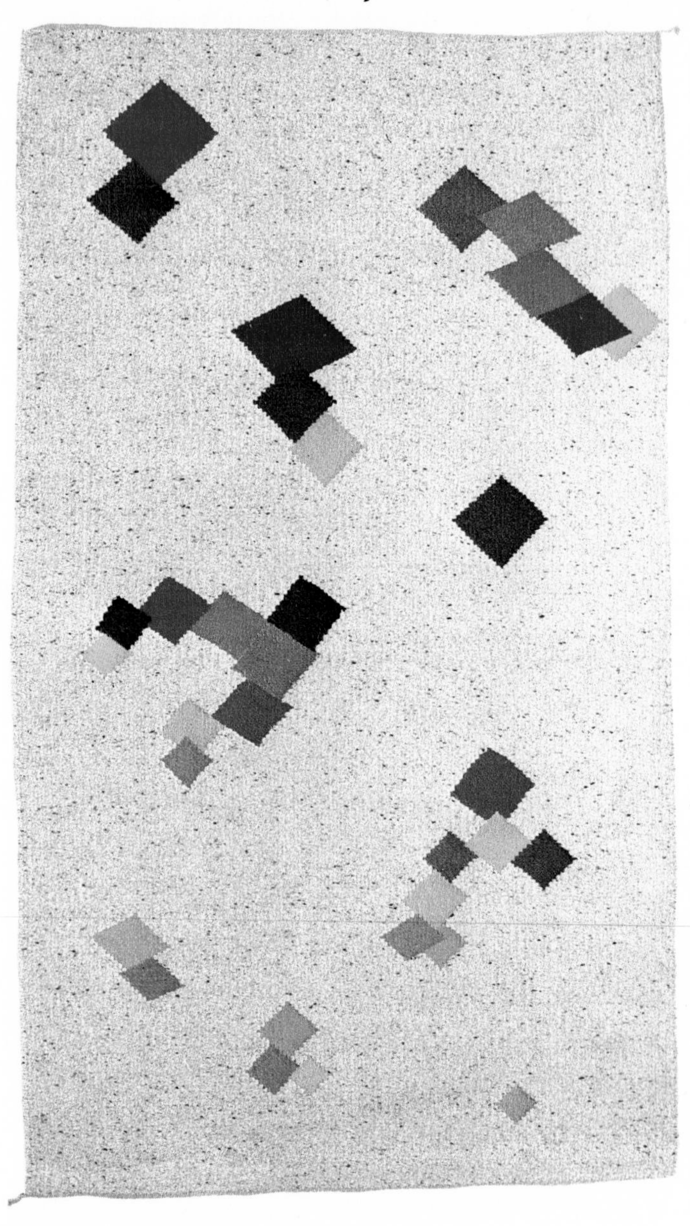

Woven rug designed to illustrate how color can convey depth, movement and rhythm on a flat surface.

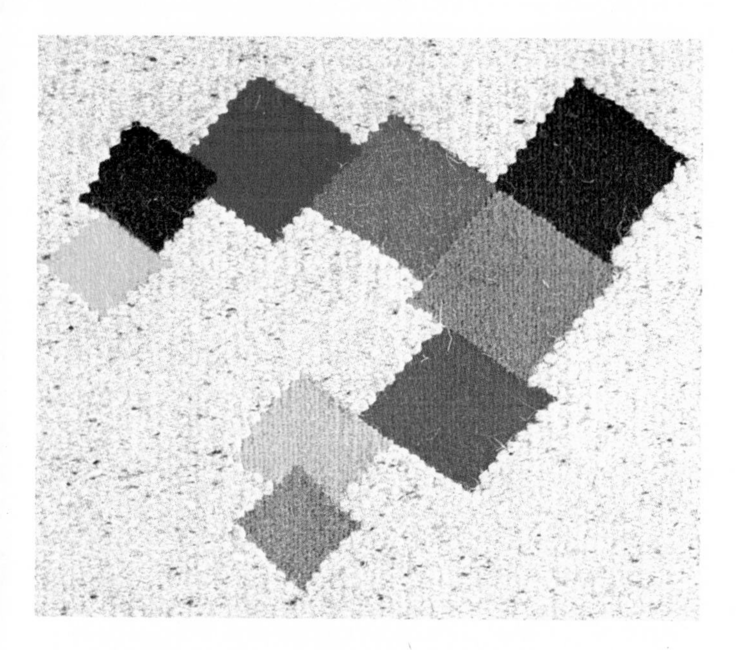

Materials Linen warp, woolen weft; thick Berber yarn was used for the background to give a textured look.

Construction Tapestry weave in small vertical slits. The diamond shapes and the background are woven together. First make bottom of diamond by weaving the background color around a "V" shape. Then fill in with a bright color, thus completing half of the diamond. To form the top part of the diamond, continue with the bright color, decreasing the warp ends being woven in each row to the peak.

Detail Represents 10% of the rug.

Rainbow doodles

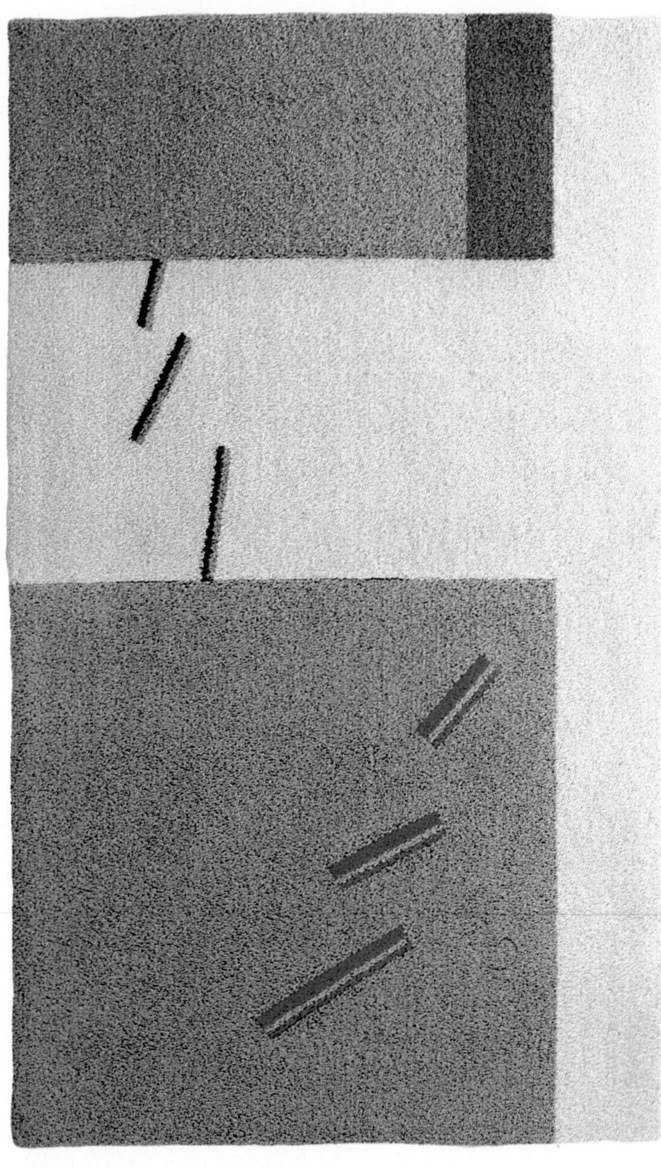

Punch hooked rug in a free-style design. The image is very simple in concept, yet the result is quite unique and pleasing. Half the fun is in drawing your own "doodles".

Construction Work the rainbow doodles first, then outline them in the background color. The edge of the rug is worked next, and finally the background.

Falling dominoes

Punch hooked rug with a sense of depth and movement in the size and positioning of the falling dominoes.

Construction The small lines (dominoes) are worked first, then outline the large squares using their own colors (green for the green, etc.), and fill in the squares. Finally outline all forms in white, and fill in the entire background.

Over the rainbow

Braided wall hanging based on a Peruvian braid design – the original braid was wrapped around the head as a turban. Here, the size of the braid is expanded by using thicker yarns and more than one element. Each three-inch (7.5-cm) element consists of two groups of "A" threads and one group of "B" threads. The groups should be arranged like this:

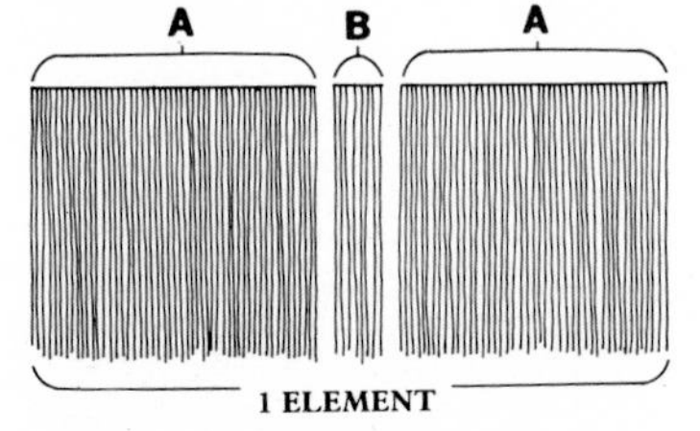

In this particular hanging, each "A" group is made up of 40 threads and each "B" group of 6 threads. As a general rule, "A" groups should be between 40 and 80 threads and "B" groups should consist of 8 threads. The large number of "A" threads gives the padded effect.

Materials The tools needed are exactly the same as those used in making the *Parallelogram*, p. 64.

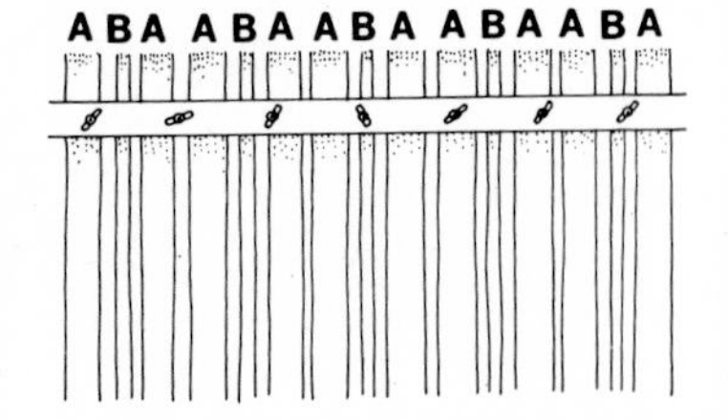

Arranging the yarns Cut the warp threads 2½ times the desired length of the finished wall hanging. Clamp the elements between the two pieces of wood halfway down the length of the threads, so that equal lengths are hanging out from either side of the clamp. Be sure to place the elements in the sequence shown in the illustration. Work with an even number of elements, such as ten or twelve. Since the width of the hanging depends on the thickness of the yarn and the number of elements, you will need a greater number of elements if using finer yarn.

Construction

1. Interlace the threads within each "B" group in a plain weave. (This will result in loose threads hanging in an upside-down "V" shape.

2. Find the two center "A" groups in the middle of the clamp. Pick up alternate threads to form an opening, or shed, in one group of "A" threads. Pull all the threads from the second "A" group through the shed. The choice of which "A" group is on top and which is pulled through is up to you and the desired finished effect. Now change the shed by taking the lower warps to the upper position and letting the upper warps drop down to the lower position.

3. Weave the four loose "B"-group threads on either side of the center through the sheds of each of the two crossed "A" groups, one thread at a time, changing the former lower warps to upper warps and vice versa every time a new "B" thread is passed through. Continue by crossing all the other "A" groups, then weaving the "B" threads through.

4. The first crosses must be done from the center out to one edge, then the center out to the other edge, but after this work from left to right, then turn the right-edge group back, and work from right to left.

5. Work appropriate groups until they meet evenly at the bottom. Sew or knot the ends together. These can be turned under later or wrapped around a rod for hanging. Re-clamp the wood over the woven part of the braid, and turn the piece around. Work second half of hanging until all groups are even at the bottom (or leave wall hanging in a "V" shape, if preferred). To reinforce, insert a strip of iron-on interfacing in the last shed between the upper and lower warps and machine-stitch across. Then pull the loose thread ends together and wrap them into tassels.

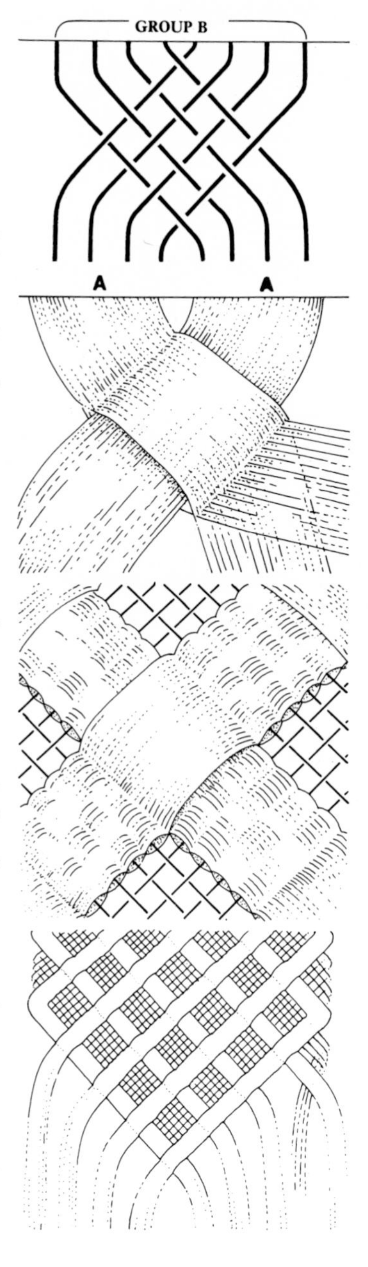

Fun Rugs

Rugs can be conversation pieces and sources of amusement, as well as being practical. Rugs such as No parking *and* Artist's palette, *both graphic representations of everyday objects, create 3-dimensional illusions. Children will especially enjoy* Snakes and ladders *as well as the brightly-colored clown rug.*

No parking

Latch hooked rug in a realistic scene from everyday life.

Materials 2-ply yarns (although varying the thickness of yarns used creates interesting effects).

Construction Latch hook overall design, keeping colors as close to the real subject matter as possible. The yellow lines are worked in a slighly higher pile than the rest of the rug, and the dark spaces in the drain were cut close to give the impression of a hole.

Clowning around

Hand hooked rug based on a child's drawing.

Materials Wool strips in bright, primary colors.

Construction The designer drew the clown directly onto the canvas, following the lines of a drawing by her granddaughter. The clown's face, as the smallest detail, should be hooked first. Outline the juggled balls with two rows of lightest background color. Fill in the background, changing direction and shades frequently to create a sense of movement. Hooking the child's name and date of the rug adds a personal and very special sentiment.

School houses

Hand hooked rug based on a traditional patchwork quilt design of the one-room school house.

Materials Wool strips.

Construction Draw one school house on graph paper, and follow this for entire rug, altering colors where desired. Keep the roofs a bit darker than the color of the houses. For doors and windows, put in accent colors, making each house different from the other. To achieve a unified look: stick to a plain background reinforced by a darker shade of the same color in the border; outline every school house in a light color; outline all doors and windows in medium brown; and use the same maroon-red color for the basements and roof separations. For variety, choose a different color for each roof, different (lighter) colors on the houses, and different accent colors for the doors and windows.

Artist's palette

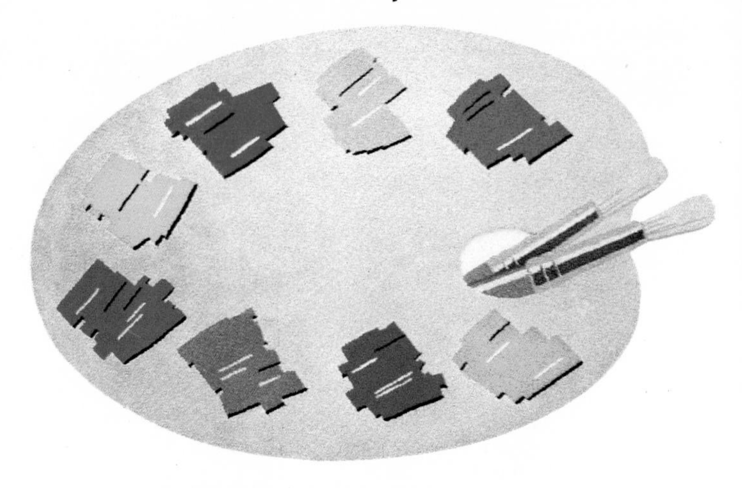

Punch hooked rug Eight different colors of "paint" on an artist's palette and two brushes placed through a real hole cut into the backing create a truly clever and unusual rug. In this design many strong colors are pulled together by a large expanse of plain background.

Materials 2-ply yarns.

Construction The blobs of paint should be worked first, followed by the brushes. Then outline all of these in the background color. Finally, fill in the background. Round and oval rugs require extra care when finishing off to ensure a neat edge. The hole in the middle should only be cut when the rug backing has been glued.

When turning back the hem of the canvas, it may be necessary to clip around curves so that the rug lies flat. Glue back the hem, then glue the entire back of the rug.

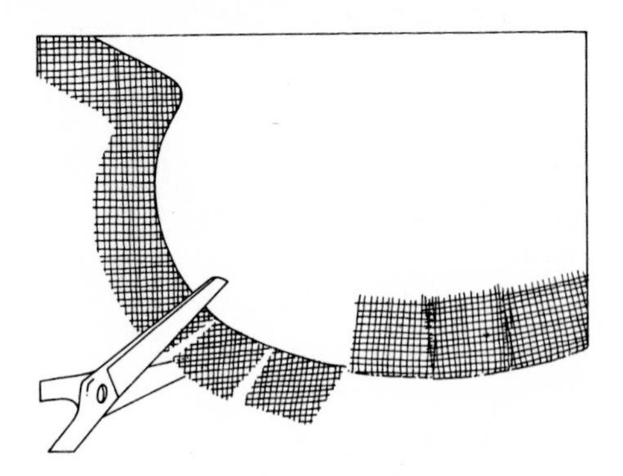

Snakes and ladders

Hand hooked rug based on the popular children's board game.

Materials Wool strips, or thick knitting yarns.

Construction Draw the pattern onto the canvas, measuring 4-in (10-cm) squares. You may prefer to stencil on numbers rather than draw them free-hand. Work black lines, then snakes, ladders and numbers. Fill in squares, alternating light and dark colors to give a checkerboard effect.

Xenophobia

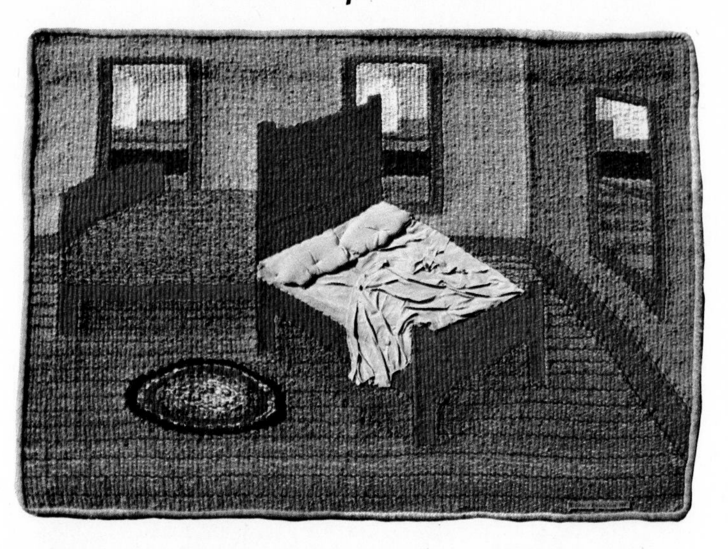

Woven wall hanging with special effects using mixed media.

Materials Tapestry wool; foam-rubber padding; small cotton cloths; acrylic paints. Edges bound with woolen fabric.

Construction Draw an outline of the desired picture in black marker on white paper. Place behind warps of weaving so that the black lines are visible during the weaving process. Fill in a specific shape by building up rows of color in that area.
To create perspective in the floor, weave fewer and fewer brown rows between the dark "cracks". Shadows under the bed are areas woven in slightly darker brown. For sheets, sew small cotton cloths to the tapestry surface over a thin foam-rubber padding, then paint sheets to keep wrinkles in place.

104 West Vernon

Woven wall hanging based on the designer's childhood home.

Materials Rug wools on linen warp.

Construction The designer first sketched a small version of the house using simple shapes and large patterned areas, and varied the sizes and colors within the design as she wove. The wall hanging is worked from the bottom to the top – the progression of weaving moving, for instance, from the brown trunk of the big tree to the grass beside it, to the bushes, patio, distant fields and the sky under the tree, before the leaves are woven in. The clapboards on the house are several rows of thick wool, then two rows of dark wool. To make the red road, weave small triangles, then "lean" brick after brick onto the slope created.

ANIMALS

From French tapestry fowls and American barnyard pigs to a family cat – these are some of the animals featured on the following pages. Realistic or stylized, primitive or sophisticated, animals appeal to everyone, and are good subject matter for rugs.

King of the jungle

American hand hooked rug, second half of nineteenth century High pile rugs such as this one were popular in the Waldoboro area of Maine. Today "Waldoboro" refers to any rug with a sculptured pile surface.

Animal squares

Needlepoint rug based on details from sixteenth century French tapestries in the Musée Cluny in Paris.

Materials Crewel wool, single canvas, 12 stitches/in.

Construction This rug is worked in 12-inch (30.5-cm) squares with four separate borders, which are stretched and joined when complete.

A hopping rabbit can be depicted on canvas by careful planning on paper first. The placement of the head and legs can make a real impact in the suggestion of movement.

Maid a-milking

Hand hooked rug in primitive style of early northern England hooked rag rugs. This quaint scene records a piece of country life long ago. The bright milkmaid's dress and yellow pail create a point of interest amidst the subtler tones of cows and landscape.

Materials Wool strips.

Construction Hook milkmaid, cow and calf first, then work the surrounding landscape, blending various colors. Fill in the large expanse of field and sky last.

Cat mat

Punch hooked rug If Kitty is an important member of your household, you may want to immortalize her by making a rug in her image. Simply follow this design, but color in the appropriate parts to match your cat.

Materials 2-ply yarns in ¼-in. (½-cm) loops.

Construction Work the small details first (outline of head, facial features, leg), then the outline of the body. Fill in areas of the body according to the colors of your cat. Then work the border, and finally, the background.

Hook this shape and add spots or stripes in places that correspond to your cat.

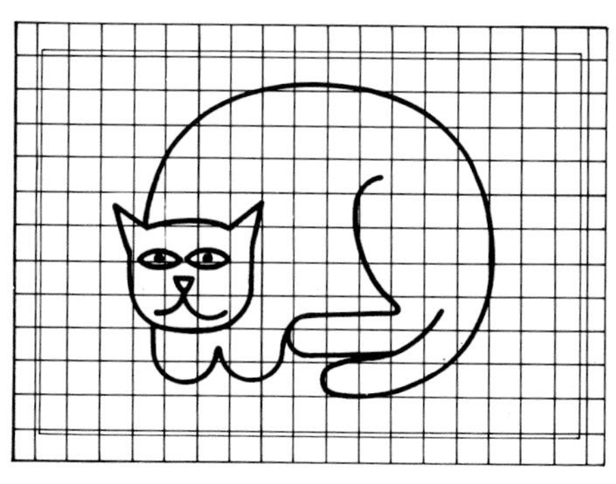

Pigs in clover

Hand hooked rug inspired by a small pig figurine the designer received as a gift.

Materials Wool strips, hand dyed to create a slightly "mottled" effect in the background.

Construction Start by hooking the front pig. Outline the snout, mouth, tail, and feet in bright red, make nostrils in darker red, fill in with pink. Next, outline the pig (ears, legs and eyelashes, too) in dark brown. Since one leg of the larger pig is in front, this must be worked before the rest of the smaller pig can be hooked. Also, complete the smaller pig's legs and right ear before hooking the rest. Finally work his left ear. For the larger pig, hook the snout, mouth and feet, then the right ear, right rear leg, left rear leg and then the body. The face and left ear can be filled in last. Outline one row of background color around the pigs, stems, leaves and flowers. Hook two or three rows all around where the background and border meet. Then fill in the background at random.

How now?

Hand hooked rug based on a drawing by the designer's daughter.

Materials Wool strips in a variety of textures.

Construction Draw the pattern on graph paper for an easy-to-follow guide. Hook the cow first. Then outline in the background color, and fill in the background. Change colors and the direction of hooking to make the background more interesting.

Children's drawings are often bold, colorful and uninhibited. No doubt any small child would delight in being presented with a rug or wall hanging based on his/her original artwork.

MATS

It seems difficult to believe that people who took so much time and effort to make pretty mats cleaned their muddy boots on them! Years ago small rugs were made for functional purposes – as hearth rugs or door mats – but today you can decide whether to place your work on the floor, or to hang it on a wall.

American hospitality

American hand hooked mat, second half nineteenth century This was probably placed at the front door as a "welcome" mat.

Full circle

Early twentieth century Welsh prodded mat probably used up many parts of old woolen clothing – nothing was ever wasted.

Materials Wool strips of any varying colors.

Construction Work small circle in the center first, then outline with another color all around. Continue adding another color for each new circle-row until the mat is the desired size. Cut out canvas around circle, leaving a few inches to turn back for hem. Glue hem to back, and apply glue to entire back to "hold" stitches, and sew on a strong backing fabric.

Home sweet home

Hand hooked welcome mat with braided border, inspired by folk art designs.

Materials Wool strips hand dyed; closely-woven wools suitable for braided border.

Construction Work from sketch or graph paper plan. Hook flowers, rabbit, cat, and other details first, filling in the background last. Using the simple braid technique, work braid long enough to fit around the entire mat. Sew the braid onto the completed mat. If you prefer not to use the mat for its original purpose, it would look especially nice if hung above a fireplace.

Shooting star

Punch hooked rug This bright and lively mat welcomes visitors in a powerful way.

Materials 2-ply yarns in ¼-in. (½-cm) loops.

Construction Work the letters first, then the outline of the shooting star. Fill in the star. Then work the border of the rug, and finally the background.

Bold round-edged letters or neatly squared ones can be drawn on the canvas to make this punch hooked rug into a "welcome" mat.

Blue braid

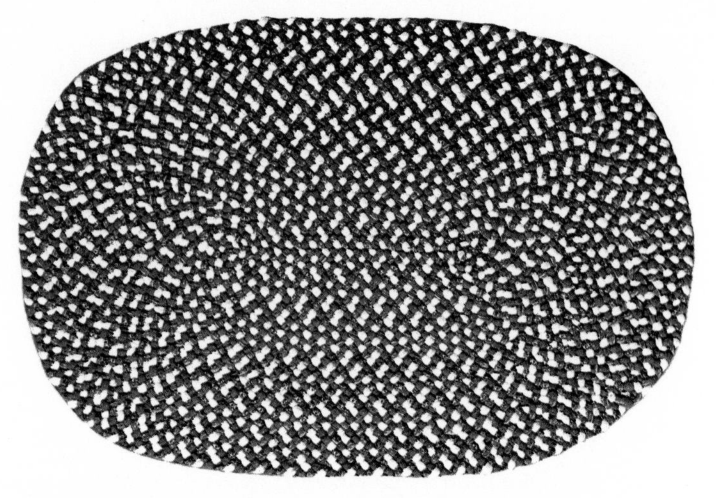

Braided mat in the traditional American braided style.

Materials 100% cotton fabric; 100% polyester quilt batting; 100% cotton cord or carpet thread and blunt-ended needle for lacing braids.

Construction Insert a polyester batting, as in *Valentine* mat, opposite. Work as a continuous braid, using basic braid technique, and shape into oval, tapering off at end.

To lace together:
Insert the needle through the first loop of the right-hand braid, without penetrating the fabric, and take it down and across to the base of the corresponding loop on the left-hand braid. Pass it up inside this loop and cross to the base of the next loop on the right-hand braid. Pull the thread tight to make the lacing as secure and as invisible as possible.

Lacing an oval shape:
Begin about halfway down the straight center braid and work downwards. When you reach the first curve, change direction and lace upwards towards the second curve. Continue around in the usual way.

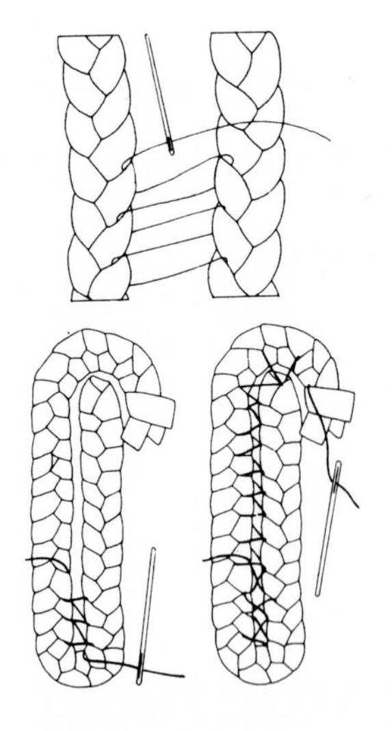

Valentine mat

Braided mat brightly exclaims its particular message.

Materials 100% cotton fabric; 100% polyester quilt batting; 100% cotton cord or carpet thread and blunt-ended needle for lacing braids.

Construction This uses a slight variation on the basic braid technique, as the cords of the braid are filled with soft polyester batting, resulting in a mat that feels thick and spongy underfoot. Simply lay the batting (cut in 1½in. (4cm) wide strips) inside the 2in. (5cm) wide strip of fabric and fold the edges of the fabric into the center. Fold again, so that the layers of material to be braided are four layers thick. (Basting the fabric edges together will help avoid any slipping or turning.) If basting stitches show in the completed work, they can be gently pulled out without damage to the mat.

To shape heart: The pointed bottom end is formed by braiding in a square "corner" shape, and the crease at the top of the heart, by braiding a reverse square "corner". Each round (single "circuit") of heart shape is braided and attached as a separate piece, with the ends butted and sewn together. Continue adding on (lacing) each separate braid around the heart, until mat is desired size.

Lacing curves:
Use the same method as straight lacing, illustrated opposite, missing out the occasional loop on the outer braid as shown. Check that the article will lie flat and if not adjust the positioning of the missed loops.

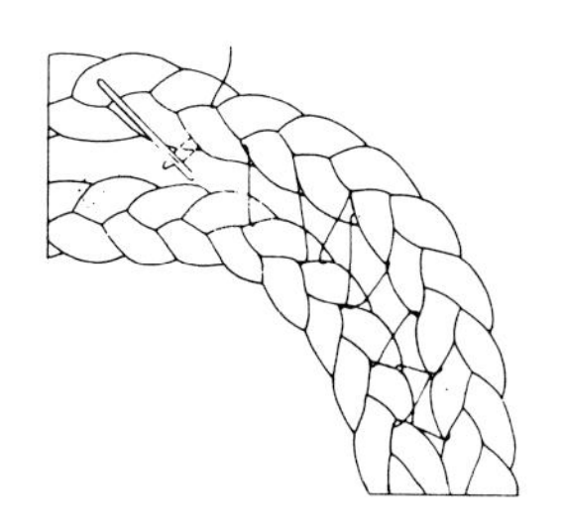

Pretty pineapples

Needlepoint rag rug with padding has a thick, spongy feel, and is not only attractive, but hard-wearing.

Materials Medium-weight cotton in 25 – 36in (63 – 90cm) long strips (approx. 16oz. (500g) for stitching, 4oz. (115g) for padding over a 16in. (40cm) square of canvas, 4oz. (115g) for stitching, 1oz. (25g) for padding over an 8in. (20cm) square of canvas); for padding use old cotton strips; size 13 tapestry needle 3in. (75mm) long; small scissors; rug canvas 3½ holes/in. (25mm). Add 4in. (10cm) to the size of the finished work for amount of canvas required; carpet tape to reinforce edge of finished mat.

Construction Cut fabric into 2in. (5cm) wide strips, cutting heavier fabrics narrower – 1½in. (4cm) wide. Cut padding strips into 1in. (2.5cm) widths. If stitching fabric is cut wide – 2½ – 2¾in. (6 – 7cm) – no padding is necessary.

Slanting stitch *As in continental needlepoint stitch, bring strip horizontally across canvas, but skip over three diagonal holes each stitch. Simply stitch over padding, placed horizontally across canvas.*

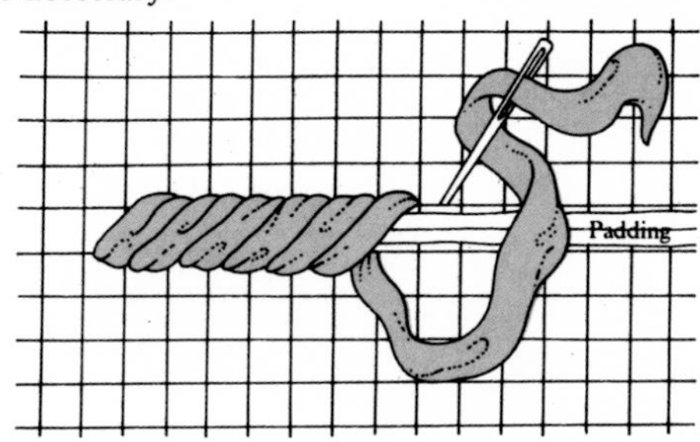

Straight stitch *(for stripes) can be worked over 2 – 5 holes, giving different stripe widths as required. First place padding strips underneath (not needed for 2-hole stitch). Use two rows of padding strips for 4- and 5-hole stitches. Simply stitch vertically from bottom to top hole, moving across canvas from left to right for first row, right to left for next. Alternating rows this way ensures that the canvas is not pulled in one direction.*

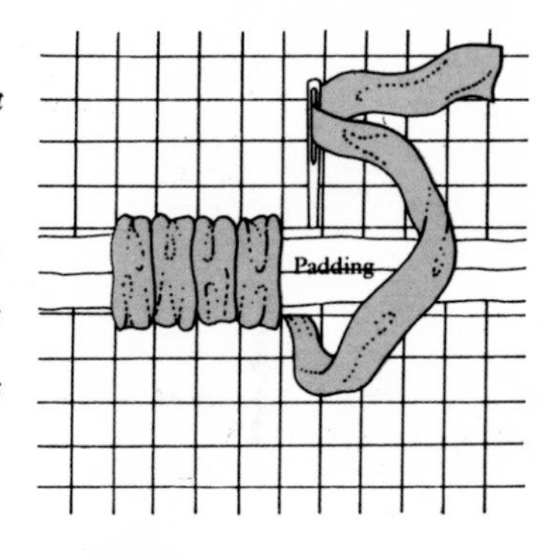

Diagonal stitch *Mark diagonal line through center of diagonal row of holes in padding strip over this line. Stitch over padding into the two holes to either side of diagonal row of holes just marked. (The first stitch is through two holes perpendicular to the adjacent row of straight stitching.)*
For the second stitch (and subsequent stitches), stitch sideways across the diagonal line. Continue to complete diagonal. A cross-stitch can be used to form lozenge shapes.

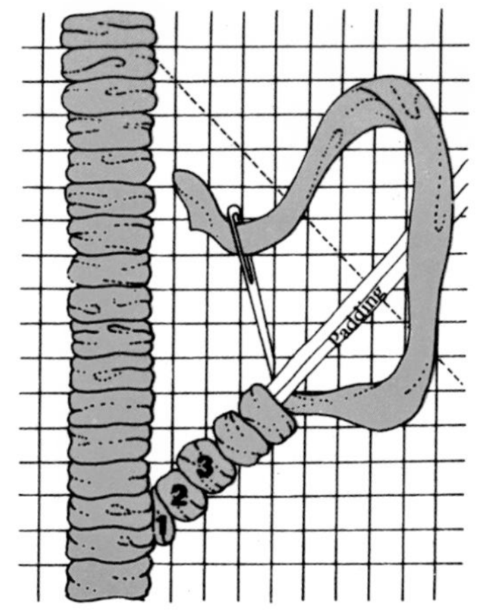

Ahhh!

Needlepoint rag seat pad Thick, bouncy and beautiful.

Materials Medium-weight fabric; cotton scraps for padding (same amounts as described in *Pretty pineapples*, p. 92); size 13 tapestry needle; small scissors; rug canvas, 3½ holes/in. (25mm).

Construction Use needlepoint stitches, as described on p. 93. Turn back edges of canvas, edge-stitch so that no visible holes are left, and apply iron-on interfacing to back. Sew on fabric backing and attach two long "ribbons" of cotton fabric to each upper edge to tie to chair.

Index

Acknowledgements

Rugs and wall hangings designed/made by
Pia Alexander 88; Wendy Barber 60; Ann Davies 24, 25, 37, 42; Elizabeth Cameron 30; Grace Erickson 59, 78, 79; Marion Ham 85; Ann Lindsay 84; Marchioness of Tavistock 28; Joan Moshimer 32, 74; Pat Nolen 90, 91; Rodrick Owen 64, 70; Mrs Paul 81; Mrs D. Passmore 26, 54; Nora Pearse 73, 77; Anna Polanski 44, 46, 66; Caroline Slinger 40, 43, 58, 72; Sarah Steen 92, 94; Rebecca Wolf 38; Patrick Vaughan 29, 62, 68, 69, 76, 83, 89; Rugs on pp. 56 and 57 were made by the disabled at Blackfriars Settlement Workshop, London. Rugs reproduced by kind permission of The American Museum in Britain 49, 50, 80, 86; Anatol Orient 44, 46, 66; Blackfriars Settlement Workshop 56, 57; Crane Gallery 48, 52; The Lake District Art Gallery and Museum Trust 82; National Museum of Wales (Welsh Folk Museum) 61, 87; Sweet Nellie, A Country Store 88, 90, 91; W.H.I. Tapestry Shop 28, 30, 34, 38, 81

Artist
John Hutchinson

Photography
Ian O'Leary

Typesetting
Cambrian Typesetters

Reproduction
Newsele SRL